FOURTH EDITION

SAVE
OUR SLIDES
PRESENTATION DESIGN THAT WORKS

WILLIAM EARNEST

Kendall Hunt
publishing company

Cover image and all interior images © Shutterstock, Inc.

Kendall Hunt
publishing company

www.kendallhunt.com
Send all inquiries to:
4050 Westmark Drive
Dubuque, IA 52004-1840

Copyright © 2007, 2010, 2013, 2016 by William Earnest

ISBN 978-1-5249-0053-3

Contents

Introduction iv

A Crime Story 1

How It All Went So Very Wrong 6

A Few Simple Rules 20

Rule 1: Templates and Themes: Choose Wisely 25

Designer's Notebook: *Templates and Themes* 38

Rule 2: Text: Reining in Wordiness 39

Exercise: *The Joy of Keywording* 46

Rule 3: Fonts: Use Sans Serif Typefaces 54

Designer's Notebook: *Fonts* 60

Rule 4: Images: Keep It Classy 61

Rule 5: Color: High Contrast 68

Exercise: *Putting It All Together* 72

Rule 6: Animation: Easy Does It 74

FAQ: *Animation* 79

Rule 7: cApiTaLIzaTiOn: Dial It Back 81

FAQ: *Capitalization* 86

Presenter's Checklist

Stand and Deliver 88

Body Talk 89

Hide and Seek 90

Video Victory 91

Auto In-correct 92

Beautiful Bookends 94

It's Transition Time 97

About the Author 100

Introduction

The name Herbert Morrison is probably not one you recognize unless you're a Jeopardy whiz, an airship aficionado, or your favorite year happens to be 1937. But you might know Morrison by the catch phrase he popularized. He was on assignment to cover the *Hindenburg's* landing in New Jersey on May 6, 1937. When instead the airship exploded and crashed in a massive cloud of fire, Morrison kept recording his report. In tears at the horrific sight playing out before his eyes, after a moment or two he screamed what would quickly become one of the most famous lines in journalism history:

"Oh, the humanity!"

© Everett Historical/Shutterstock.com

Almost 80 years later, "Oh, the humanity!" remains widely used as a form of parody to re-cast everyday mishaps as full-fledged, world-class "disasters."

Like similar phrases from history (such as "a day that shall live in infamy"), out of respect for its origin, it's only employed to describe faux tragedies, not real ones. *The Simpsons* used the line when the show's own version of the *Hindenburg*—the Duff Beer blimp—crashed into a radio tower and explodes. And *Seinfeld* used it when Newman's mail truck caught fire.

So when it comes to the millions of bad slideshows out there—watched by tens of millions of people every day, there really is only one thing to say: *"Oh, the humanity!"*

Or in proper 21st century parlance: #ohthehumanity

A Crime Story

Bad slides aren't against the law (if only), but judging by their reputation, one might think they constitute their own category of "crimes against humanity." Consider the following headlines and excerpts collected from stories over the last 15 years:

"PowerPoint is Evil"
—WIRED

"We have met the enemy and he is PowerPoint"
—THE NEW YORK TIMES

"Physicists, Generals And CEOs Agree: Ditch The PowerPoint"
—NATIONAL PUBLIC RADIO

"the PowerPoint presentation has become synonymous with dull"
—BBC

"Digital slideshows are the scourge of education"
—SLATE.COM

PowerPoint gets blamed by name more than other programs, but that's just because it's an easy target. It's been around longer and still dominates the market (most estimates give it a 95% share). In reality, Prezi and Keynote are just as susceptible to bad design.

So what exactly is going on here? Even at the height of their use, earlier communication technologies such as flip charts and overhead projectors (using transparencies) were never objects of such fear and loathing as has been visited upon digital slides.

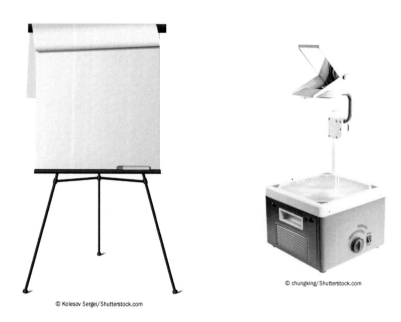

© Kolesov Sergei/Shutterstock.com

© chungking/Shutterstock.com

Not surprisingly, I haz a theory about that.

Perhaps it's because—even at their worst—flip charts and overhead projectors were never guilty of the kind of communication crimes that have been committed with digital slides. If speakers screwed up with flip charts and overhead projectors, their offenses were basically misdemeanors. What's been done with digital slides are felonies by comparison.

In the interest of making the most of this jurisprudence metaphor, how about a formal reading of the charges? You may have committed some of these errors yourself, but you've certainly sat through every single one of them as an audience member—not just once or twice but many, many, many times.

There are probably a few more violations, but the 15 on this list cover the majority of them. Not to mention, they fit perfectly on that clipboard graphic.

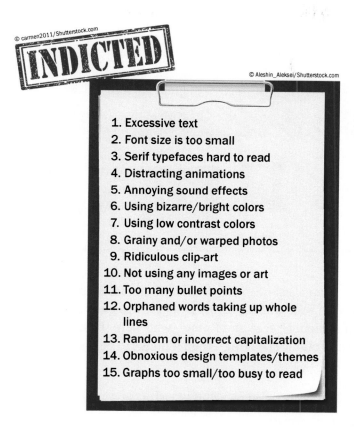

© carmen2011/Shutterstock.com

© Aleshin_Aleksei/Shutterstock.com

1. Excessive text
2. Font size is too small
3. Serif typefaces hard to read
4. Distracting animations
5. Annoying sound effects
6. Using bizarre/bright colors
7. Using low contrast colors
8. Grainy and/or warped photos
9. Ridiculous clip-art
10. Not using any images or art
11. Too many bullet points
12. Orphaned words taking up whole lines
13. Random or incorrect capitalization
14. Obnoxious design templates/themes
15. Graphs too small/too busy to read

Complete or not, it's one heckuva list. And these problems aren't limited to PowerPoint. We've all seen the same issues pop up over and over again in Keynote and Prezi.

Is it any wonder that audiences are sick of bad slides?

This question brings us to the root cause of the entire problem. In all of our typing and pointing and clicking, we've forgotten the single most important principle of all good communication, whether slide-based or not: **It's always about the audience**.

© Andrey_Popov/Shutterstock.com

And it always has been. Aristotle preached it (*Rhetoric*, Book II) as did Cicero (in the second book of *De Oratore*). So if it was good enough for the rhetors of ancient Greece and Rome—who were the first ones to systematically study public speaking—then it ought to be good enough for us.

© Panos Karas/Shutterstock.com

ARISTOTLE

"People always think well of speeches adapted to, and reflecting, their own character ..."

Aristotle, *Rhetoric* 2.13, 1390a, trans. Roberts

© Cris Foto/Shutterstock.com

CICERO

"For a cause requires that the expectations of the audience should be met with all possible expedition …"

Cicero, *De Oratore*, 2.77.313, trans. Watson

In subsequent chapters, we'll revisit the 15-count indictment of bad slide design and offer specific remedies for each offense.

But before we do that, it's worth taking a little historical detour to help us understand just how this communication crime story unfolded. The sage advice of ancient rhetors stood us in good stead for nearly 2,500 years. Then, in less than two decades, the sudden dominance of all things digital seems to have undone everything the collective wisdom of the ages had taught us about giving speeches.

By the way, Plato didn't even trust *paper*. Imagine what he'd think of our slides.

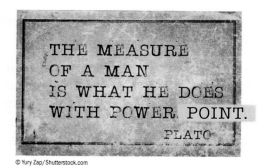

THE MEASURE
OF A MAN
IS WHAT HE DOES
WITH POWER POINT.
PLATO

© Yury Zap/Shutterstock.com

How It All Went So Very Wrong

When it comes to designing and presenting with slides, we're in nothing less than a fine mess. And that's the bad news, though it's not news at all to anyone interested in this book. The good news is that we can use clues to reconstruct what happened. The sordid tale of our presentational decline is the story this chapter will briefly recount.

But the even-better news is that we *can* fix what's wrong, and it doesn't involve getting rid of slidemaking software or resurrecting a 50-year-old overhead projector (good luck finding bulbs anyway). The remaining chapters of this book are devoted to describing the cure for what ails us. Spoiler alert: It's *good design*. Not exactly rocket science, but based on the millions of bad presentations we endure every day, it seems almost as mysterious and inaccessible.

© Marzolino/Shutterstock.com

© donatas1205/Shutterstock.com

Now then, to history. We're going to set our WABAC Machine (or, rather, this clever Steampunk WABAC knockoff) to around 400 B.C., right smack-dab in the middle of Greece's Golden Age. Sadly, we can't linger here. Just long enough to note that Plato (at left) looks suspiciously like Leonardo Da Vinci in this drawing. And of course to point out that he (Plato) and the other orators of ancient Greece relied on **mind and memory,** had no charts or note cards, and still got a lot of remarkable s____ done. This was true for several centuries' worth of Greek rhetors, from household names like Isocrates and Demosthenes to also-rans like Aristotle and Socrates.

In addition to throwing parties the likes of which no one has witnessed before or since, Roman society placed a premium on skillful oration. As is the case with Aristotle's proofs, Cicero's canons of rhetoric are still taught in many persuasion and public speaking courses. Just to put that in perspective, Aristotle died almost 2,340 years ago and Cicero a cool 2,060.

From Speaker to Audience: The Direct Model

What made classical orators so successful and gave their techniques such staying power? Because they developed and perfected the **direct model** of public speaking—a transaction that went in a straight line from the speaker's face to the faces of audience members, eye-to-eye. Like this:

© skvoor/ Shutterstock.com

No notes

No script

No slides

No props

No muss

No fuss

☑ Eyes

☑ Voice

☑ Body

☑ Brain

Writing had been around for a while, but Plato considered it a crutch. Like him, most classical orators felt that speaking and writing were **two separate domains**. They all did tons of writing, mind you, and they also spoke their brains out. But it never seemed natural or logical to them to combine the two.

By contrast, we modern humans have spent the last couple of centuries combining them in ever-increasing ways. So much so that talking without notes or a manuscript or some other form of writing (slides, for example) seems as strange to us as it no doubt seemed natural to our ancient friends. It's to our detriment that we've largely lost the use of the direct model of communication. If you really want to impress people, **just talk to them**.

For example, when it came to light that President Obama relies on teleprompters

© Jose Gil/Shutterstock.com

most of the time, he caught a lot of flak. It had been largely assumed that his remarkable speaking style was direct and unscripted. Since almost all modern politicians use teleprompters, the impression that he didn't need one was a refreshing change of pace. The news that he not only used them, but used them far more than any previous president became fodder for Obama's detractors. "It's a negative because it's a sign of inauthenticity. It's a sign that you can't speak on your own two feet," Republican media strategist Fred Davis told *The Washington Post*.

Whether such a critique is fundamentally fair or not, perception is reality when it comes to audience reaction and public opinion. You're simply more persuasive when you speak without notes of any kind, but especially when you ditch the electronics. U.S. Representative Michele Bachmann found this out the hard way. During her response to President Obama's State of the Union Address in January 2011, the position of the teleprompter caused her to look into the wrong camera for the entire six-minute speech. This

© Morphart Creation/Shutterstock.com

incident and a series of other public-speaking gaffes did significant damage to her upcoming presidential campaign, which never gained traction despite six months of effort and more than $10.5 million in donations.

But let's back up a bit (about 500 years). If we park the WABAC at the year 1500 and look out across time in both directions, it's clear that we've landed at a turning point in human history.

From Memory to Media

The world prior to 1500 is one in which writing was time-consuming and done mostly by hand. Above all, it had almost nothing to do with the art of speaking. But from about 1500 on, the rise of mechanical printing gave greater and greater importance to paper as a means of communication. In one of the great seismic shifts that human culture has known, **orality** began to be supplanted by **literacy**.

The widespread use of paper and printing introduced a new kind of communication transaction—an indirect one. In this **indirect model**, speakers and audiences are joined by a third entity: **a physical medium**. For you trivia buffs, the Latin root of medium is *medius*, which literally means "middle." So, technically speaking, media is something that *gets in the middle of* speakers and their audiences.

So there were still speakers, there were still audiences, but now something had come between them. Hmmm, what could possibly go wrong? (Actually, with paper not that much. Just wait 'til we get to electricity). Over time, speakers got accustomed to the idea of using media (especially paper),

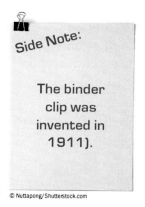

Side Note:

The binder clip was invented in 1911).

and doing so began to seem quite natural. This became truer than ever once the Industrial Revolution had reshaped the world yet again by the end of the 19th century.

But imagine Plato asking, "Where's my speech?" as though it were something that could or should exist outside his own head. To borrow my favorite line from "The Princess Bride"—inconceivable!

As the 19th century turned into the 20th, speakers increasingly relied on paper as the source of their words. This shift to paper made speech-making considerably easier for speakers because they no longer had to rely on memory. But from the standpoint of the audience, it may have felt like a demotion.

At least a little. Something else was now *competing with them* for the speaker's undivided attention. What had been a solid, unbroken line between speaker and audience, like this: ⎯⎯⎯⎯⎯⎯

… was now "dotted" with occasional (or worse) **glances at some intervening type of media**. That media was mostly still paper, with the eventual addition of overhead projectors and 35mm slides.

As developments go, this shift to media instead of solely using one's mind is not insignificant. **Breaking eye contact** with the audience **to refer to your notes** builds into the public speaking transaction the **potential for disconnect**. This disconnection might be momentary (which audiences could tolerate) or longish (much more awkward) and it could happen any number of times during a speech— depending on the speaker's abilities.

© Zern Liew/Shutterstock.com

Then in the 1920s and '30s, QWERTY typewriters did for paper as a medium what microwave popcorn did for snacks in the '80s. Speakers clacked away typing speech notes, outlines, and manuscripts by the millions. As early as 1935, the introduction of *electric* typewriters began to make it easier than ever to type a whole speech verbatim. The electric typewriter was ubiquitous in the '60s, '70s, and '80s as IBM's Selectric machines became essential tools in virtually every kind of organization. In the economic and technological boom that followed WWII ('50s, '60s, early '70s), speakers acquired additional forms of media for their presentations. Flip charts, overhead projectors, transparencies, and 35mm slide projector systems became commonplace.

Slides, Slides Everywhere

But especially the slides.

© Tatana Popova/Shutterstock.com

In the working world (corporations, nonprofits, government agencies, education), almost no institution or organization was without them. The "audio-visual" era had officially begun, and 35mm slides quickly became the koine of the realm of presentations—the "language" that everybody spoke. Slide projectors were so wildly popular, in fact, that they managed to accomplish what the chalkboard, flip chart, and overhead projector never could, to "cross over" to the other side (of the economy)— the coveted and very lucrative consumer market.

It was primarily Kodak and its Carousel line of projectors that brought 35mm slides to the domestic masses (*Mad Men* fans may remember it from the Season 1 finale). Businesses and other institutions often used expensive, high-end slide projector systems manufactured not only by Kodak, but also Agfa, Electrosonic, Bell & Howell, Elmo, GAF, Minolta, Nikon, and dozens of other manufacturers you never heard of (such as Hasselblad, Inox, Pentacon, Prestinox, Pouva, Reflecta, and—I wish I was making up this last one—Filmoli).

In short, slides and projectors were everywhere—businesses, offices, schools, churches, community centers. Now they were even in your aunt and uncle's basement in Nebraska (which, if you were lucky, also had a pool table and comfy oversized armchairs).

Kodak alone sold more than 19 million Carousels according to media studies scholars like Paige Sarlin. The company produced them continuously for 40 years, all the way up until the middle of 2004.

And they were popular for lots of good reasons. Slides were "as easy or difficult to make as you liked" and projectors "as easy or hard to use as you liked," wrote Peter Lloyd in *AV Magazine*. In the business world, he noted, "no high-level product launch was considered complete without a multi-image presentation that used at least six projectors and 500 slides."

So if your company rolled out a fancy new portable 8-track cassette player in the 1970s, it was worth the thousands (or tens of thousands) of dollars you spent creating the audio-visual extravaganza that introduced it to the world. 35mm slide presentations could do just about anything. And if it

was done right, it was possible to create a truly impressive "multi-image" presentation, with synchronized soundtrack, visual fades and dissolves, and even the illusion of motion. Business presentations on this scale were nothing less than works of art.

Boykov/Shutterstock.com

But simplicity ruled the day for most presenters, who didn't have the budgets for such grand productions, and who didn't need them anyway. Speakers who knew their material could use a few 35mm slides to illustrate their talking points, and nothing else was needed.

And so what if the room was dark? At least that way it'd be more obvious if audience members were looking at their smartphones (had they existed then) instead of the speaker. Dimming the lights for a speech or presentation meant something important was about to happen—or at least something interesting.

© rudall30/Shutterstock.com

Call it a "sense of occasion." Whatever you call it, one thing is clear: In today's world of electronic slides, we seem to have lost it.

The Great Disconnect

Recall our previous notion of **media** as something that **comes between** (gets in the middle of) speaker and audience. Recall too that, by definition, using media (instead of just mind and memory) introduces *the potential for* **moments of disconnection** between speaker and audience. It doesn't mean it *will* happen, just that it *could*. If they were using paper, speakers *could* bury their heads in their manuscripts and read their speeches verbatim instead of delivering them in a natural, engaging style. Fortunately, that didn't happen often. The best speakers knew their material well enough that they only had to glance down at their manuscripts occasionally. And a *quick glance* every now and again was and is just fine with most audiences on most occasions.

But unlike the use of paper, in the world of 35mm slides/projectors, audiences and speakers weren't meant to look at each other anyway, but at a shared screen instead. In the history of public speaking, this was a big change in the way things had been done for centuries (with the exception of the Magic Lantern era—for more on that, see p. 14).

Overhead projectors and transparencies used the same premise, but were inferior versions of the idea. If you've never had to give a presentation using an overhead projector, be grateful. It was hard to deliver a really engaging presentation that way. Most of the time, watching people write words by hand using color markers was not nearly as much fun as it sounds. If you were lucky, they had good handwriting (or could afford to laser print their transparencies). And it was hell on left-handed people (smudge city).

High art it was not. By comparison, even the humble chalkboard was a better choice. Assuming there were other options available, the best presenters simply stayed away from overheads and transparencies altogether. The possibility of disconnecting with the audience was far greater with overheads/transparencies than with paper or slides. One explanation for this could be that the former were too easy to use. Little time, energy, or skill was needed. Not so with 35mm slides.

Seriously. It took *effort* to create an old-school slideshow. Instead of just scribbling words on a transparency, you had to *make* slides. And that often started by grabbing your 35mm camera (leather case optional), shooting the photographs, getting them developed, re-shooting if necessary, and, finally, getting them produced in slide format.

© fotosutra/Shutterstock.com

So you really had to think about what you were doing, and …

you
had
to
think
visually

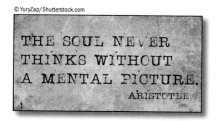
© YuryZap/Shutterstock.com

THE SOUL NEVER
THINKS WITHOUT
A MENTAL PICTURE.
ARISTOTLE

And *that*, ladies and gentlemen, is the **key to everything**. People think in pictures and ideas, not words. That's why the era of 35mm slides was so successful. If a speaker used slides, then:

© ConstantinosZ/Shutterstock.com

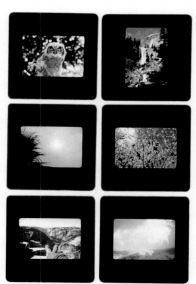

most of the time, in
most situations,
most slides were pictures

© VikaSuh/Shutterstock.com

© trekandshoot/Shutterstock.com

As in photographs. Images taken by a camera. The only reason anyone ever made slides was because they wanted to **show photos on a big screen**.

Illustrated Lectures

Projection screens (or a nice big wall) have always been meant to display photographs and other types of images. That's just as true in today's digital age as it was in the era of the Magic Lantern (1650–1910). In those days, slides were made of *glass*, the images were initially hand-painted, and the light source was some kind of *flame*.

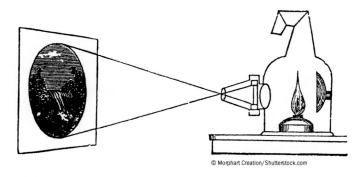

© Morphart Creation/Shutterstock.com

As the predecessor to movies, Magic Lanterns were often used to entertain, delight, or frighten audiences. But as the predecessor to 35mm slides, they were also used in education, business, and civic life for delivering, as Dr. Terry Borton calls it, "illustrated lectures." Blog excerpts from the Museum of the History of Science, Technology and Medicine at The University of Leeds paint the history of this period in even more detail:

> ... use of visual aids was common. In school classrooms, a popular way of incorporating these was to give each pupil a lantern slide and ask them to prepare a talk about it, which they delivered while the image was projected ... In churches, lanterns were used during services or Sunday school classes ...

SOURCE: https://museumofhstm.wordpress.com/tag/magic-lanterns/

35mm slide shows did the same kinds of things, but on a vastly larger scale. Whether Magic Lantern or 35mm, slides provided an easy way of **telling stories visually**, a kind of "narrated sight-seeing." Big screens (or the nearest wall) provided the sights and speakers supplied the narration.

As photography, film, and electricity came of age together in the early 20th century, the Magic Lantern began to give way (after a reign of 350 years) to more modern methods of image projection—motion pictures and photographic slides made from sheets or rolls of film.

First introduced in 1936 (so close), 35mm slides were made by:

1. **Taking pictures with a 35mm camera**

2. **Getting the film developed**

> **Interesting Side Note:** Until they got sued and lost in the 1950s, only Kodak could develop the film and you had to pay for that up front, when you bought the film.

© Laborant/Shutterstock.com

3. **Cutting up the individual exposures (i.e. photographs) directly from the strips of developed film,** and

© Lenscap Photography/
Shutterstock.com

4. **Mounting them as is into a 2" x 2" cardboard or plastic frame**

Still a lot of work, but with all that time and money on the line, it's easy to understand why the results were often spectacular. This was particularly true after the introduction of Kodachrome II film in 1961, regarded as a vast improvement over the 1936 version. Of course, it should come as no surprise that Kodak's slide business made billions.

The Visual Model

As this history makes clear, "slides" are nothing new, even though we tend to think of them strictly in the modern, completely digital sense. Instead, we should think about it like this:

Slides 1.0	Magic Lantern	1650 to early 1920s
Slides 2.0	35mm projection	1930s to early 1990s
Slides 3.0	Digital slideware	Mid-1990s to present

Today's electronic slides are just the most recent version of what began with the Magic Lantern and 35mm slide shows. From a communication standpoint, Slides 1.0 and Slides 2.0 used the same basic presentation formula that, in theory at least, we use today: <u>Speaker and audience sharing images projected on a screen</u>, perhaps accompanied by live sound and other special effects.

Again, the idea is the illustrated lecture. Or, illustrated *talk* if the word "lecture" seems too outdated. The second word doesn't really matter. It's the first word—*illustrated*—that's key.

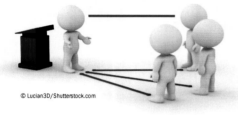

© Lucian3D/Shutterstock.com

Modified by Kendall Hunt Publishing Company

Even in the **direct model** of communication (at left) the best speakers are still *illustrating* their ideas—it's just that they're doing it with their words rather than actual images.

In the **indirect model** shown here at right, good presenters are still illustrating their ideas, but they're using written words or notes to help them remember what they want to say. As we discussed beginning on p. 8, this is less than ideal, because it interrupts the speaker's direct line of sight with the audience, splitting

Clipboard: © Mr.Creaâtive/ Shutterstock.com

© Lucian3D/Shutterstock.com

Modified by Kendall Hunt Publishing Company

her/his attention between the notes and the listeners. This split attention means that there are at least some moments of disconnection. But the best speakers keep those moments short and infrequent, giving as much of their attention as possible to the audience.

The introduction of slides (1.0 and 2.0) made an interesting alteration to the basic public speaking transaction. Instead of being strictly a direct or indirect model of communication, it becomes instead a **visual model**.

© VoodooDot/Shutterstock.com

In this visual model, speakers and audiences no longer need a direct line of site. Speakers become **narrators** and audience members become **viewers** in addition to listeners. They <u>listen</u> to the speaker but <u>look</u> at the screen. And instead of looking *at* the audience, speakers look *with* the audience, at a shared screen.

In the (g)olden days of Slides 1.0 and Slides 2.0, audiences seemed quite capable of splitting their attention between the screen and the speaker's words. They could give their eyes to one while still lending their ears to the other. Remember, it was mostly dark during those presentations. It had to be for the Magic Lantern to work (lights down, just like in a movie theater). And all but the most expensive 35mm slide systems weren't bright enough to work well unless the lights were dimmed or off altogether. Most of the projectors in that era rarely went above 1,200 lumens. In a well-lit room, you need to get into the 2,000 to 3,000 range to avoid washing out the screen. It wasn't until the digital era (late '90s on) that powerful projectors became plentiful (and affordable).

© Javier Brosch/Shutterstock.com

Slides 3.0

But in order for the visual model to succeed, there's one other important detail: WHAT'S ON THAT SCREEN REALLY MATTERS. So much so, in fact, the rest of this book is devoted to it.

But before we get to that, I'll let Robert Gaskins tell you why Slides 3.0 has been such a communication disaster. Gaskins was one of the original inventors of PowerPoint®, back when it was used for making slides and transparencies, before Microsoft bought it. In 2007 he wrote a beautiful reflection on his invention at its 20th anniversary, and his perspective may be surprising to some. In the decade from 1992 to 2002, he notes that the digital revolution in computers and projectors brought an end to the era of 35mm slides and overhead projectors. These things either disappeared entirely from conference rooms and classrooms, or else they just sat there gathering dust. It was a brave new world of presentations, but:

> ... presenters had no limitation and increasingly no firm intuition as to what was appropriate ... They tried adding elements from multimedia shows (such as sound effects, attention-grabbing transitions between slides, moving text, and bullet points that "flew" to their places from somewhere off screen). ... virtually none of the extraneous entertainment had any purpose or benefit in the kinds of meetings where overheads had been used. Successive versions of PowerPoint made these elaborate features easier and more tempting to use ...
>
> SOURCE: COMMUNICATIONS OF THE ACM, DECEMBER 2007/VOL. 50, No. 12

In other words, slides started to look like more like **advertising**, and that's putting it mildly. We all know what most slide presentations (regardless of the brand) look like for the most part.

35mm slides were easy to produce from photographs. Creating slides with text on them was computer-intensive and time-intensive (in other words, expen$ive). So speakers rarely did it. When they did, it was often to put title slides between sections of the presentation. If they needed to use a lot of text, they just left the lights on and used overhead projectors instead. Slide shows were for meant for visual consumption and for listening, not for reading.

Digital technology has made it possible for something very strange to happen: **Paper and screen have merged**. Paper used to be for words. Screens used to be for images (plus a little text as needed for annotation). Not anymore. Welcome to Slides 3.0.

© Pavel L Photo and Video/Shutterstock.com

Where speakers are irrelevant. You see, we don't need them anymore because we can just read everything they're saying right on the screen! When presenters do this (and they do it a lot), they create two competing channels of information: (1) The speaker's words in the air, and (2) the speaker's words on the screen.

This arrangement is a deeply flawed formula for communication—speakers doing their thing, audiences doing theirs, and never the twain shall meet. Words should be used to conjure mental images in the audience, not displayed on screen in place of those images.

But this flawed formula can be fixed, and that fix begins by throwing away your keyboard. Not literally of course, but do set it aside and learn to use it sparingly when working on slides—with one exception: Use it as much as you want to type in search terms for images and artwork. The keyboard is the wrong tool for making slides; it's like trying to paint with a hammer.

© robtek/Shutterstock.com

© Elnur/
Shutterstock.com

Your tool of choice should be the mouse. If you're using it, then almost by definition, you're thinking visually. And you need to think visually in order to make effective slides. Even text—to the extent that you use it—is more likely to be rendered in a visual style, the way it would be on a highway sign or a well-designed billboard.

Today's slides need to function the way slides used to—the way they did from 1650 to about 1995 during Slides 1.0 and 2.0. They work best when they're used to manage information visually. And text? The perfect vehicle for managing text is and always has been paper.

But don't tell Plato.

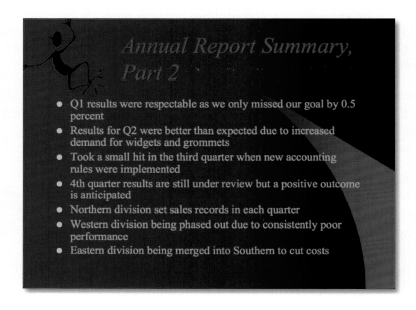

A Few Simple Rules

Presentation slides have become the most misused tool in the history of communication—which is why this book is **not** another user manual for slide software. There are too many of those already, and look where they've gotten us:

That's where this book is different than most. It's about how to craft **better** slides by learning some useful **rules of design**. Because a slide like this isn't just ugly and off-putting—it's bad communication. It's as though it were designed to obfuscate meaning rather than convey a message. Here's a quick analogy. Take a look at the following sentence. All the information to make a meaningful sentence is present, but it's put together wrong:

```
the jumped fox cow quickly brown over
```

Extracting meaning from a sentence like this is no easy task. And this is the case despite the fact that you're already quite familiar with the popular sample sentence it's based on. A sentence written with no sense of the syntax rules that inform the language it's using—so poorly designed that it isn't even functional—is intolerable. But many of the presentation slides we see on a daily basis are just as flawed. From the standpoint of effective communication, they're like this one—their "visual syntax" is all screwed up. In visual media, bad communication often stems from poor design.

But don't throw away your old slides. Recycle (or remodel) them using the rules of good design described in this book.

So, turn on the computer and get out a pen—today is the first day of the rest of your slides.

© Talvi/Shutterstock.com

The world of digital slides is sort of the Wild West of communication:

- No laws
- No judges
- No roads
- Lousy maps and charts
- Too many bullets

All the West needed to tame it was some good old-fashioned law and order—Judge Roy Bean and a calvary contingent or two, plus a few permits here and there. Basically, rules.

Ever since they became popular in the 1990s, slideware programs—despite their tremendous potential for creative communication—have become a kind of electronic wilderness that we've all gotten lost in. What we need to set things right is a straightforward set of do's and don'ts—**a few simple rules**.

I don't mean to traumatize you, but let's go back once more to that loathsome slide we looked at a couple pages ago. We can all agree that we *hate* slides like this, right?

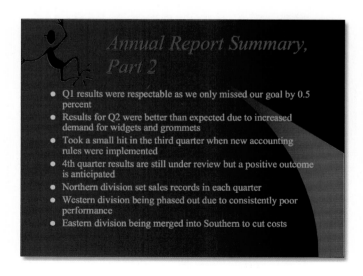

But do we know why? After all, we can't fix it if we can't clearly describe what's wrong with it in the first place. So let's start there.

From the standpoint of good design—design that helps rather than hinders the process of communication—here's the official indictment:

- a shifting shade of sleep-inducing "electric" blue
- a template older than most computers
- text that's too small to read
- a font better suited for printing than on-screen display
- tired, cheesy clip-art (some clip-art is perfectly fine; this isn't)
- poor color contrast
- annoying animation and sound effects (trust me, they're there)
- too many bullet points

And way, (way, way) too many words. No wonder we're all sick and tired of slide-based presentations. Fortunately (and this is really, *really* important) **none of these problems is inherent in the software programs themselves**.

Not a single one. Instead, what we're seeing is the result of misuse. In other words, it's user error—at least technically. The truth is that we're not really to blame since no one ever taught us this stuff.

In that spirit, I'd like to offer seven **Rules of Design** for presentation slides (i.e., slides that are intended for big screen use in front of a roomful of people). Follow these rules and your audience is far more likely to react favorably to what you're pitching (or at least stay awake—and possibly even pay attention).

We'll start with a simple list, then drill down for more detail as we go through the remaining chapters.

The Rules of Design for slides are:

1 **TEMPLATES and THEMES:** Choose wisely

2 **TEXT:** Reining in Wordiness

3 **FONTS:** Use Sans Serif Typefaces

4 **IMAGES:** Keep It Classy

5 **COLOR:** High Contrast

6 **ANIMATION:** Easy Does It

7 **CAPITALIZATION:** Dial It Back

Seriously. You gotta stop with the capitalization thing.

In the coming pages, each of these Rules of Design will be defined, explained, and illustrated in detail.

And because you'll continue to use electronic slides for many years to come, I've included a couple of **"Designer's Notebook"** entries. These pages allow you to write down the names of preferred templates and fonts. The idea is to build a repertoire of reliable tools so that, as time goes by, you can develop and refine an enviable design style that is uniquely yours.

Rule 1: Templates and Themes

Choose Wisely

Not all slideware templates (also called "themes") are created equal. Templates of course are those ready-made design schemes that are included with the software.

When it comes to picking the right template, about 90% of the battle is knowing which ones **not** to use. But we'll start with the following general features that separate good themes from the riff-raff:

Desirable Template Features

- Light background color (the preferred choice)
- Uniform background color (no shifts in brightness or shade)
- Complementary, inconspicuous design elements

Not surprisingly, the telltale characteristics of bad design themes are pretty much the opposite of these. But some are worth mentioning specifically:

Bad Template Characteristics

- Bright or medium shades of **blue**
- Medium-colored backgrounds of any hue
- Backgrounds shifting from light to dark or vice versa
- Clunk, ugly, or otherwise distracting design elements
- Any theme that has grown stale from overuse

The last item on that list is worth some elaboration. There are decent themes/designs that are simply overused, and for that reason alone should be avoided. Examples include Dad's Tie, Melancholy, and Cloud Skipper as well as newer themes like Civic and Concourse. If you see a theme that's used all the time, then it's probably time to choose another design.

Lists like the two preceding ones are great, but nothing brings them to life like a good set of examples. And since the bad stuff's always more fun, that's where we'll go first. You've heard of the five people you meet in Heaven? Well, this is not that list. Instead, I give you the:

5 Templates from **Hell**

Of course, there are many, **many** other design themes out there that are just as bad as (or worse than) these. But these are worth pointing out because they teach at least two valuable lessons:

1. For reasons that defy explanation, they continue to be widely used today, numbing audiences the world over and helping to reinforce slideware's bad reputation.

2. They effectively illustrate the characteristic problems that all bad templates share. So if you come across a template that reminds you of one of these five Templates from Hell, drop what you're doing and run screaming from the room.

⊘ Soaring

Save Our Slides

Meet the oldest template in the world. There's no better way to look unoriginal and stale. Just how many shades of blue can we use at one time? And what is that "swoosh" thing?

Seriously, *Soaring* was one of the original PowerPoint templates. It hasn't shipped with a new version of the software since Bill Clinton was in his first term as president. Yet somehow it lives on, the veritable cockroach of templates.

So I'll give it this much—it's got staying power. But unless you want to turn your audience into a raging mob of bored zombies, you shouldn't give it the time of day.

⊘ Whirlpool

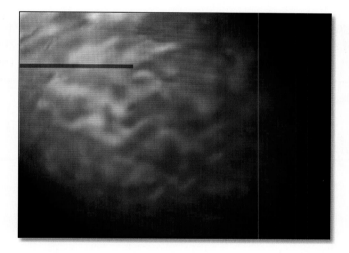

Ever wonder what the core of a nuclear reactor looks like? Or the left lobe of your brain? How about both at once? Well, now you know. Nightmarish and disturbing, your content can't compete with all that noise in the background. So much for whirlpools being "relaxing."

⊘ High Voltage

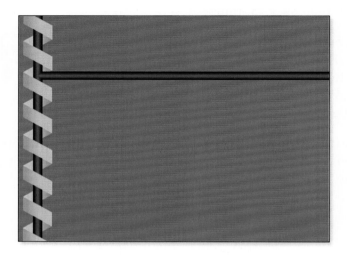

Ah, the 1950s. Mad scientists, DNA, and shades of blue so dreary that they went out of style in, well, the '50s. And even though you can't see it here, don't forget about the best part: A "particle" that flies up the side tube then cuts across—on each and every new slide you open. Audiences looooove stuff like that.

⊘ Marble

Rough day at the mausoleum, dear? Not even a mortician could make this one look good. More detailed than a Seurat painting, it may capture your audience's attention, but will always do so at the expense of your content (and their interest). Always.

⊘ Blue Diagonal

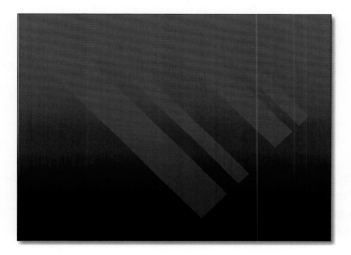

Just what the world needs—another funky blue template. An old, overused one too. Not to mention the gradient shift from extremely bright to nearly black. With so many strikes against it, you'd think it would be mighty unpopular. But you'd be wrong.

Some Better Choices

The news isn't all gloom and doom though. Many of the newer design themes seem to have gotten things just right.

Following are a few of my personal favorites. Most of these templates are versatile enough to be used in a wide variety of presentational settings, from the classroom to the boardroom.

☑ Bold Stripes

This design proves that blue can work quite well as an *accent* color on a template (using it as the whole background is the problem). The vertical pinstripes give this template a dash of subtle elegance. It may be "bold" but it's not overpowering.

☑ Network

Not much to it, is there? And that's the beauty of it. A good template is present but unobtrusive—a time-honored design principle known as *transparency*. Such templates will always let you and your content be the proper stars of the show.

☑ Profile

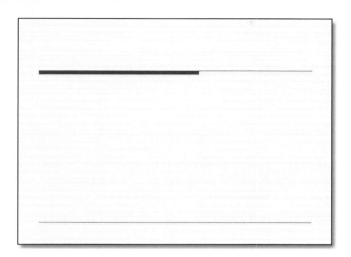

They don't display accurately here in print (above), but this template has light gray pinstripes running horizontally (below).

Like *Bold Stripes*, this one is elegant and professional, but with a splash or two of red for a little added personality. I still use this one a lot in my classroom lectures.

☑ Echo

Three dots and a line? You're probably thinking, *Well I could have designed that.* Yeah, me too. And indeed we could have. Good templates don't have to be complex or difficult to create. The only hard work is the conceptual stuff—knowing what constitutes good design in the first place.

☑ Eclipse

Think of this one as the preceding *Echo*'s more extroverted alter ego. And if the color scheme's not your cup of tea, it's easily changed via the **Slide**

Master function (or its equivalent, depending on the program you're using).

☑ Layers

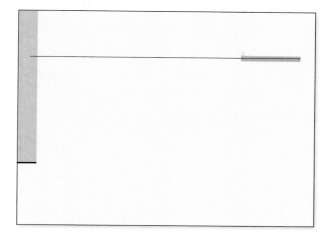

One of my all-time favorites. You'll want to change the default font for *Layers* to a sans serif typeface (the focus of Rule 3). This template's more upscale than most, making it a good choice in no-nonsense, serious, or sophisticated settings.

☑ Level

As with *Layers*, the default typestyle needs to be changed from serif to sans serif. And if earth tones aren't your thing (or it isn't harvest time yet) just change the colors of the various elements to match your specific needs.

BYOD (Design)

To illustrate how easy it is to customize any template to better suit your particular presentation's requirements, read on.

Here's another good template, which happens to be called *Edge*. By any measure, it's pretty unassuming. If you need a low-key or straightforward quality, this is your ticket.

Templates like *Edge* can quickly be transformed from Plain Jane to Cinderella in just a few clicks. As noted previously, go to the menu and choose the **Slide Master** function under the **View** menu (in PowerPoint).

Once the Slide Master is open, changing things to better suit your needs couldn't be easier:

1. **Double-click on the upper gold line to change its color to whatever you want**

2. **Do the same with the lower gold line (or is it more of a mustard color?)**

3. **Insert your organization's logo or other art work, and you're all set**

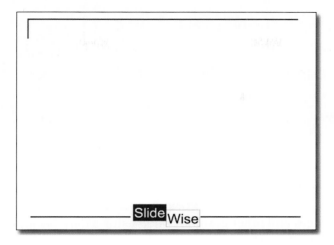

As was the case with the bad templates we looked at, there are of course many, many more good ones than the few shown here. But the ones mentioned here admirably illustrate the qualities that all effective template designs share. And like the changes to *Edge* shown here, most design themes can be easily transformed through a few simple edits using the Slide Master function.

Can't find all of these templates or looking to corral a few more? A Google search should lead you to many of these old favorites, and you should definitely take a few minutes to review the templates available on templates.office.com.

One thing you've probably noticed about these good templates is how lightly-colored the backgrounds are. That's because in most venues, **dark text on top of a light background** offers the greatest readability for the audience.

Again, that's true in most venues, but not necessarily all. Here's a list of several situations in which you might consider using a dark background template (with light-colored text):

When Dark Templates Might Work

- The room is going to be very brightly lit

- The screen has lights shining directly on it

- A light background doesn't fit the mood you need

- You want to use the organization's colors but they look ghastly against a light background

Don't get me wrong. I've seen some stunning presentations that used dark backgrounds, but in general it takes much more work to achieve results that rival what can be done with a light background. For example, it's harder to work with images and other graphics when using a dark background color (more on that in Rule 4).

If you have to use a dark background, below are three templates that you might want to consider (remember to use a *light* color for the text).

These are three of many possible choices, but they represent the genre well. Notice that the backgrounds are composed of solid colors (no shifts in brightness) even if more than one color is used. Additional design elements are present as well (lines, etc.), but they complement rather than distract.

☑ Circuit

☑ Refined and Vapor Trail

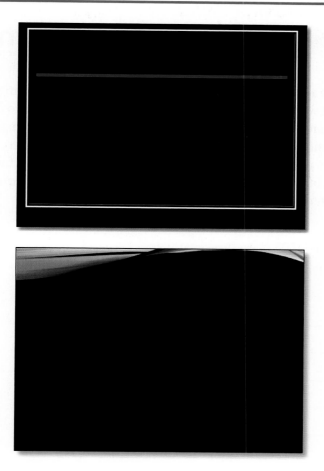

Take a moment to open PowerPoint and browse the available templates. Everyone still refers to them as "templates" but they are now officially known as "themes." Whatever you choose to call them, they can be found under the Design menu heading. Revisit the various choices based on the perspective you've gained from reading this chapter. As with all the Rules of Design, after you've used them for a while, making good choices will become second nature. In the meantime, to help you keep track of templates you particularly like, a Designer's Notebook entry is included on the next page.

Templates and Themes

As you come across good templates (or bad ones), keep a running list here of what works and what doesn't. Fill in or circle the stars to denote favorites. That way, five years from now when you're hammering out that career-making presentation for some big wigs at your office, you won't have to try to remember the name of that perfect template you found once upon a time but lost track of. What was it called again—*Astronaut? Waldorf Astoria? Asteroid?*

Good Templates

	Favorite		Favorite
_____	☆	_____	☆
_____	☆	_____	☆
_____	☆	_____	☆
_____	☆	_____	☆
_____	☆	_____	☆
_____	☆	_____	☆
_____	☆	_____	☆
_____	☆	_____	☆
_____	☆	_____	☆
_____	☆	_____	☆

Avoid Because of Overuse

_____   _____   _____

_____   _____   _____

_____   _____   _____

Rule 2: Text

Reining in Wordiness

Rule 2 is one of those principles that can be summed up in a single sentence—a single sentence that every presenter should have to write on a chalkboard 500 times when they first get into the slide game:

© Runrun2/Shutterstock.com

PowerPoint is not a word processor
PowerPoint is not a word processor
PowerPoint is not a word processor
PowerPoint is not a word processor
PowerPoint is not a word processor
PowerPoint is not a word processor
PowerPoint is not a word processor
PowerPoint is not a word processor
PowerPoint is not a word processor

In other words, **PowerPoint is not a word processor**. Design guru Edward Tufte describes slideware as a "low-resolution" medium, meaning that dense objects like text get lost easily. And he's exactly right. In this regard, slides are no different than a highway sign or a billboard. And when was the last time you saw a highway sign that looked like this?

> Austin is the next exit. Soooo, yeah. If that's your destination, you should probably get in the right-hand lane and activate your turn signal.

By the time you're finished reading such a sign, you will have done one or both of the following:

- missed your exit
- wrecked the car

No transportation official interested in a long-term career would ever dream of misusing the road sign medium in such a ridiculous fashion—and yet we do it with slides all the time. Of course we know that in reality the same sign would probably look more like this:

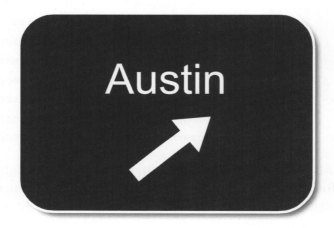

The #1 problem with PowerPoint is our tendency to put **too many words on slides**. If your need for text is great, use Microsoft Word instead and give your audience handouts to read. It's a much better fit, and they'll thank you for it. To sum up:

- PowerPoint is a **visual** medium
- MS Word is **textual**
- They serve different communication functions

Effective communication is about effectively managing information. And not all information is the same, which makes it critical to pick the medium that is best suited for the kind of information you're trying to convey. Lots of words? Paper. Got information that would translate well to big-screen visuals? Slides.

Here are some helpful ideas for limiting the number of words on a slide. There are actually five separate strategies that can help stem this epidemic of "verbal diarrhea," otherwise known as verbalitis. Don't try these on an empty stomach, and be sure to drink plenty of water.

Top 5 Ways to Cure **Verbalitis**

1. Reduce sentences to key words
2. Aim for ≤ 20 words per slide
3. Keep type sizes large enough to read
4. Use accepted symbols & abbreviations
5. List no more than 6 main bullets per slide

© ayzek/Shutterstock.com

Let's illustrate each of these strategies in turn.

 © broukoid/
Shutterstock.com
1. Reduce sentences to key words

Consider the following, all-too-typical slide. It's certainly got a bad case of verbalitis (although you've probably seen worse).

● ● ● | **Summary of Benefits Changes for the New 2006 Fiscal Year**

○ From now on, physicals will be required in order to increase the amount of life insurance coverage, except for new enrollees

○ No physical is required when requesting a decrease in life insurance coverage

○ Pre-existing conditions will no longer be covered for new enrollees, including dependents

○ List of pre-existing conditions available in benefits packet material or from HMO website

---

If you consider the negative communication effects of such slides, then you've put your finger on the heart of what is most hateful about slideware.

After all, here's a slide that:

- is comprised almost entirely of text words
- has too many words (68 of them, to be exact)
- has absolutely no images or graphics
- treats text strictly as paragraphs, using no visual logic

One problem at a time, obviously, so in this part of the discussion we're going to concentrate solely on reducing the number of words, specifically by using the technique of **keywording**.

There's a simple formula you can use to reduce full sentences down to their key ideas. Apply the following to the title and each bullet:

ELIMINATE:

- **articles** (*a, an, the*)
- **understood pronouns/possessives** (*we, you, your*)
- **simple verbs & infinitives**
- **repetitive phrasing**

An example will illustrate just how easy this is to do. Imagine that you're the president of Acme Grocery pitching the company's home delivery service to an audience of prospective clients. Here's your main "benefits" slide:

The Acme Grocery Pledge

► We promise to offer you only the freshest produce available

► We unconditionally guarantee your complete and total satisfaction

► We will deliver your groceries to you anywhere, anytime

Now let's apply the four steps of the keywording process and see what can be eliminated:

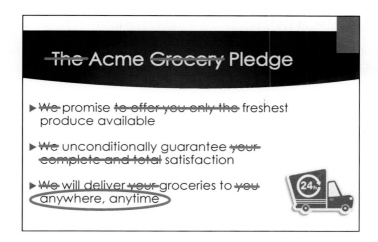

Note that the phrase "anywhere, anytime" is circled because—while important as an idea and selling point—the wording is repetitive.

Looking at this edited version, the essence of the ideas begins to come clearly into focus. We realize we can probably eliminate another word or two (e.g., "pledge" and "promise" are synonyms). Then we spy an opportunity for **parallel phrasing** (always a good idea when various ideas are of equal importance):

In short, here's where our edits have taken us:

What started with **31** words ended up with **8**

If you're keeping score, that's a reduction in verbiage of **74%**

In the process, the main selling points became dramatically clearer—
a principle so important that it's worth putting in a colored box:

> In **visual** media, **more** words does **not** equal **better**
> communication. Less is almost always more.

As a presenter, you should still **speak all the words** that were on the
original version of the slide. When presenters do this, their spoken words
will perfectly complement the key words their audiences see.

The principle of keywording
is so central to good slide
design that it's impossible
to achieve success without
it. You can do everything
else right, but if you get
this one thing wrong then
the whole show is off.

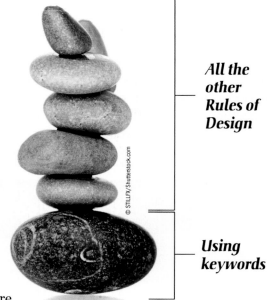

*All the
other
Rules of
Design*

© STILLFX/Shutterstock.com

*Using
keywords*

In effect, keywording is the
cornerstone of good design. Or at the very least, as
this picture suggests, it's
the **foundation** of good
design.

That's why text management
and verbalitis in general get more
ink on these pages than any other
aspect of design. And without the judicious use of keywording, of course,
there is no such thing as text management in the first place—only text
mismanagement. So reining in word count really does hinge on this one
principle.

© barbar34/Shutterstock.com

By the way, I tried to find a picture of an actual, honest-to-goodness cornerstone to use in this discussion but it just wasn't happening. During my search I came across the stack of pebbles on the previous page and it was then that I decided to switch metaphors. I'm glad I did, but I'd still like to find a descent, generic picture of a cornerstone someday.

As a consolation prize, however, I stumbled upon this picture of the Greek Parthenon. There has to be a cornerstone in here somewhere.

All rock-based metaphors aside, the keywording principle has a number of practical implications that are worth creating yet another colored box for:

- Slides are only a speaker's notes (i.e., main ideas)

- Slides are not a verbatim transcript

- No full sentences on slides except for direct quotations

- If speakers have to read from their slides, they're probably using too many words

- Slides are not a diary; speakers should be selective about what they ask the audience to look at

On that note, check out the following exercise. It'll give you a chance to put your money where your keywords are.

The Joy of Keywording

Consider the following slide, which obviously has a severe case of verbalitis.

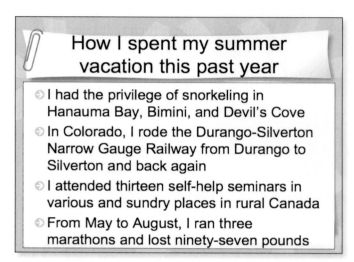

How I spent my summer vacation this past year

- I had the privilege of snorkeling in Hanauma Bay, Bimini, and Devil's Cove
- In Colorado, I rode the Durango-Silverton Narrow Gauge Railway from Durango to Silverton and back again
- I attended thirteen self-help seminars in various and sundry places in rural Canada
- From May to August, I ran three marathons and lost ninety-seven pounds

Use the strategies described in this chapter to pare down the verbiage on this slide to its essential keywords. Do this in a two-pass process, first on the blank slide labeled Draft 1 (for obvious cuts) and then on Draft 2 (for further revisions). Don't forget to fix the slide's title in addition to the body text.

As you edit, keep three things in mind:

1. It's **okay** to change words and phrases if needed

2. It **ain't** okay to change or obscure the original meaning

3. If it helps, include visually logical elements such as:

   a. sub-bullets

   b. symbols/numbers in place of words (see p. 50)

Draft 1—Obvious cuts

Draft 2—Additional refinements

2. Aim for ≤ 20 words per slide

Now let's go back to our first verbalitis patient from a few pages back—the boring one with all those words:

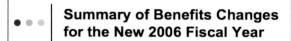

Summary of Benefits Changes for the New 2006 Fiscal Year

o From now on, physicals will be required in order to increase the amount of life insurance coverage, except for new enrollees

o No physical is required when requesting a decrease in life insurance coverage

o Pre-existing conditions will no longer be covered for new enrollees, including dependents

o List of pre-existing conditions available in benefits packet material or from HMO website

68 Words

Through the magic of keywording, we can now see our way clear of traps like using full sentences. Instead, we begin to consciously edit ourselves, choosing to **visually emphasize only what matters most** about each of our ideas.

FY06 Changes

o **increase** in life coverage requires physical exam
  • exception: new enrollees

o **decrease** in life coverage – no physical required

o pre-existing conditions not covered for:
  • new enrollees (including dependents)
  • list of conditions in packet & HMO website

36 Words

The target range of ≤ 20 words per slide turns out to be a handy metric. It provides a realistic goal that works particularly well when you find yourself editing someone else's slides. In this case, going from 68 words to 36 (rather than 20) is still a dramatic improvement.

When creating your own slides from scratch, however, try to restrict yourself to the official limit of ≤ 20 words per slide. In fact, in classes my students have consistently produced their best slides—creative, memorable, and visually appealing—when I require them to use **no more than 15** words on a slide.

If that sounds impossible to you, it's because you're stuck in word processor mode. Reboot and remember that slides are a visual medium.

 ## 3. Keep type sizes large enough to read

One of the reasons we tend to put too many words on slides is that we choose type sizes that are in fact too small for use on large projection screens. And since nature abhors a vacuum, we **type, type, type** to fill up all that empty space.

Words sized at 10 or 12 points may look perfectly fine to us as we sit at our high-resolution laptop or desktop monitors, but big presentation screens operate at decidedly lower resolutions than their smaller counterparts.

Technical explanations aside, here's the bottom line when it comes to sizing text for big screen audiences:

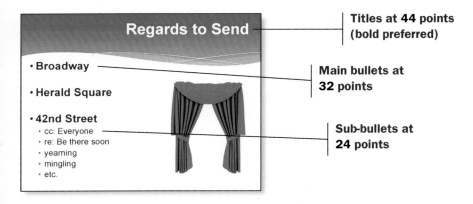

Strive for these target point sizes. Not only do they make it easier for audiences to read what's on the screen, **they place natural limits on the number of words presenters will be able to type in the first place**.

It is virtually impossible for big screen audiences to easily process text that is rendered in sizes less than 18 points. Under no circumstances should you drop below that threshold. Consider it an absolute limit. Text displayed at less than 18 points is meant to be read on paper, not projected on screen. Remember: PowerPoint is not a word processor.

4. Use accepted symbols & abbreviations

This one's pretty much common sense, but it's worth pointing out because we still see many instances where speakers forget to use it. The rule is simple. If there's a **commonly-accepted** symbol, acronym, or abbreviation for a word or phrase, then use it.

Remember, on-screen space is limited, so the more visual real estate you can conserve the better. Every character counts.

Instead of:	Use:
One, two, three …	1, 2, 3 …
First, second, third …	1st, 2nd, 3rd …
Quarter 1, quarter 2 …	Q1, Q2 …
Fiscal year	FY
Thousands	000s
U.S. dollars	USD
Number	# or No.
And	&
Street, Avenue …	St., Ave. …
International	Int'l.
Incorporated	Inc.
For example, et cetera …	e.g., etc. …
Television, compact disc …	TV, CD …
Texas, California, Maine …	TX, CA, ME …
Central Intelligence Agency …	CIA, FBI, NASA, UCLA …
Intelligence Quotient …	IQ, DNA, rpm, mph, mpg …
Martin Luther King, Jr. …	MLK, LBJ, JFK, FDR …

Familiar objects

Organizations known by their acronyms

Everyday acronyms

Historical abbreviations

And so on and so forth. I realize you don't need anyone to teach you common symbols and abbreviations. The point of including them here is simply to **remind you to do it**.

5. List no more than 6 main bullets per slide

In fact, 3, 4, or 5 bullets is better, with plenty of white space in between for a little visual breathing room.

Here's the thing. It's something of an axiom in educational psychology that the average person can retain a maximum of five to seven items in short term memory. After that, things start getting lost.

Hence, it's best not to push our luck (or, more to the point, our audience's luck). Aim for **3 to 5** main bullets, and if you can't do that, make a cold stop at **6** no matter what.

A simple test will illustrate why these numbers represent a natural barrier. Mentally study the following bullet list for a minute or so (take as long as you want), until you feel comfortable that you've got it memorized.

FY12 HR Goals

- Improve employee retention strategies

- Review sabbatical policy proposal

- Expand 401(k) investment choices

- Increase ESOP limits

- Remodel daycare facility

- Hire new foodservice contractor

When you're ready, hide this page or flip it under and go to the next one. **Do not look back**. It wouldn't be cheating, but you might miss the point of the exercise.

Okay, proceed to the next page.

Without referring back to the slide on the previous page, write down as many of the bullet items as you can recall:

_____

_____

_____

_____

_____

_____

_____

_____

_____

One last question: How many bullet points were there in total? _____

Okay, now go back and check your answers against the original.

Odds are that you didn't get the whole list correct, a reality that has several implications:

1. **You're perfectly normal**

2. **That was "only" 6 things**

3. **Which is why the upper limit is 5 to 7 items**

4. **Think about how often we see slides with 10 or more bullets!**

5. **Yikes. It's an epidemic of verbalitis.**

Note that **sub-bullets** are a different matter. We're not counting them against our total of 6 main bullets. At the same time, if a couple of main bullets have subs below them—AND you're using the proper point sizes for text—there's no way you're going to fit 6 *main* bullets into that space in the first place. This is what is known as a "self-correcting problem." See for yourself:

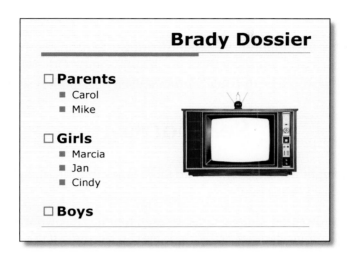

See? You can't even fit the whole Brady Bunch on a single slide. And if you thought Chez Brady was bad, try fitting the entire Walton clan on one. It just can't be done.

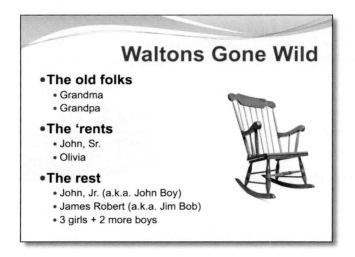

Rule 3: **Fonts**

Use Sans Serif Typefaces

Think about your handwriting for a moment. You know how you do that cute little thing with your Ys and people are always saying your Cs look like Os?

Well, fonts are to computers what handwriting is to people—we use them to give electronic type a consistently uniform appearance. Otherwise, imagine how difficult it would be to visually process even the simplest sentences:

See Spot run.

Granted, it might make a poem or two more enjoyable, but imagine having to read *War and Peace* that way.

Like your handwriting's idiosyncrasies, each font has its own way of doing things, with unique characteristics that set it apart from all the other fonts in the world. As a result, some are more appealing and more useful than others. In fact, a handful are just downright—I guess you could call them "specialized."

This one's called Linotext

Perfect for the Halloween edition of your company newsletter, but not exactly the Honda Civic of typestyles. Which is what we want for our slides—the font equivalent of the Civic:

- practical
- popular
- efficient
- not overly noticeable

And just as with cars, knowing what we need in a font makes the process of choosing the right one a whole lot easier.

54

Save Our Slides

So, if the Civic were a font, what would it look like? Simple not fancy, with nice, clean lines.

Fortunately, there's a whole class of fonts that fit this description—they're called *sans serif*. "Sans" is Latin for "without" and "serif" rhymes with "sheriff."

So what are serifs? And why don't we want them hanging around our fonts?

ser • if *n.* **The flourishes at the ends of a letter's main strokes**

See for yourself. They're not all marked here, but you get the idea.

Here's the thing about serifs. They're great in small-scale printed media like newspapers, magazines, and novels, where the type is typically tiny. In such situations, serifs provide a level of detail that helps the human eye "lock on." Sort of like visual handlebars.

But as the media changes and the type gets larger, and certainly by the time you get to something on the scale of a street sign, highway sign, billboard— or **big screen presentation**—those previously-handy serifs are now just a whole lot of visual noise. What we need on screen is **simplicity**. Clean, even lines with no fancy endings. Like so:

Mmtg

This is why you never see street signs, highway signs, or even most billboards printed in anything other than a sans serif typeface. Think about it. Which kind of highway sign formatting do we usually see?

Save Our Slides

This?   **Or this?**

Los Angeles   **Los Angeles**

Next 137 exits   **Next 137 exits**

Almost always the one on the right of course. Why, then, does the text on our slides so often look like this:

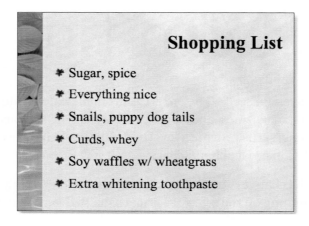

Instead of **this**?

Sans serif fonts are considerably more readable on-screen than those in the **serif** category. See for yourself:

- pick one of your own slides and make copies to work with

- render one copy in a **sans serif** font and the other in **serif** (see the handy lists on the next page)

- run the slideshow on a full-size presentation screen

- switch back and forth between the two versions of the slide

- view them from various distances and in different lighting

- invite your colleagues in and get their opinions

- celebrate Vanessa's birthday now that everyone's here

Some of the most common typefaces in both categories are displayed below and on the next page. Remember, the serif fonts will look good here because the printed page is their medium of choice. But put them on a big screen presentation and something gets lost in translation.

Popular Serif Fonts

Times New Roman   Aa Bb Cc 1 2 3 $ % &

Bookman Oldstyle   Aa Bb Cc 1 2 3 $ % &

Garamond   Aa Bb Cc 1 2 3 $ % &

Georgia   Aa Bb Cc 1 2 3 $ % &

Palatino   Aa Bb Cc 1 2 3 $ % &

Century Schoolbook   Aa Bb Cc 1 2 3 $ % &

The most popular **sans serif** faces—and therefore our **best choices for onscreen legibility**—are the ones shown here:

Popular Sans Serif Fonts

Arial   Aa Bb Cc 1 2 3 $ % &

Arial Narrow   Aa Bb Cc 1 2 3 $ % &

Avant Garde   Aa Bb Cc 1 2 3 $ % &

News Gothic   Aa Bb Cc 1 2 3 $ % &

Tahoma   Aa Bb Cc 1 2 3 $ % &

Trebuchet MS   Aa Bb Cc 1 2 3 $ % &

Verdana   Aa Bb Cc 1 2 3 $ % &

Those last two sans serif fonts are interesting animals. For its part, **Trebuchet** is by far the fanciest out of this standard stable of sans serif typefaces. While its characters don't feature serifs per se, I think it's fair to say that Trebuchet is a font with latent serif tendencies (not that there's anything wrong with that). It's a great choice when your slides need a little more jazz or sophistication than usual.

Verdana, meanwhile, is extremely readable on screen, but its characters are ginormous. Letter for letter, Verdana takes up more horizontal real estate than almost any other font. But then again choosing it is a great way to inoculate your slides against verbalitis. **Bonus tip:** Use 10-point Verdana regular (not bold) as your default font for email. It's hard to find anything clearer or more readable on the small screen.

If you must use a serif font for some compelling, unavoidable reason, then your best bet might be **Georgia** (which happens to be the font you're reading right now). It is among the most legible of serif fonts on screen as well as paper, and for good reason—Microsoft commissioned its creation specifically for that purpose.

If used, serif typefaces are best displayed at large point sizes. Hence, one practical use for them is in **slide titles**, where they can provide an added touch of elegance if desired, as in this example:

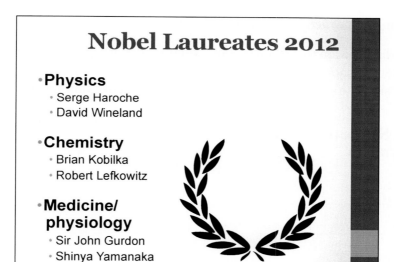

On the following page is another Designer's Notebook diary, one that lets you record the names of the preferred sans serif typefaces you come across in your slidemaking travels. There are literally thousands of typefaces out there, so it's a good idea to keep tabs on your faves.

Fonts

New fonts hit the electronic marketplace every week. Some are good, some are bad, and some are just ugly. Problem is, there are so many out there that it's hard to keep track of them all. To make matters worse, it seems that no two computers in the world have exactly the same set of fonts installed on them. (I can't actually prove that, but I'm sure it's true).

As we discussed in this chapter, **sans serif** fonts are the best choice for onscreen readability. Use this page to keep a working list of the best screen fonts you come across. If you like, use the stars to mark your favorites.

Best Screen Fonts
(sans serif)

	Favorite		*Favorite*
_____	☆	_____	☆
_____	☆	_____	☆
_____	☆	_____	☆
_____	☆	_____	☆
_____	☆	_____	☆
_____	☆	_____	☆
_____	☆	_____	☆
_____	☆	_____	☆
_____	☆	_____	☆
_____	☆	_____	☆
_____	☆	_____	☆

Rule 4: **Images**

Keep It Classy

I used to open this chapter with a spectacular showcase: The Clip-Art Hall of Shame. But, truth be told, people have a good sense of what works and what doesn't. Plus, clip-art and other images have improved dramatically in quality and number since the early days of slideware. Today there are literally hundreds of thousands of excellent alternatives to this kind of schlock.

The best rule of thumb to follow is simply "Be picky." Have some standards and stick to them. AND be willing to devote a significant amount of time to scouring the Internet for just the right image. Since slides are a visual medium, the energy devoted to conceptualizing and locating pictures or clip-art should be substantial. And the word "conceptualizing" is used deliberately—always start by looking in your mind's eye first, then go on a Web hunt to try to track down those mental images.

One of the best sources is still Microsoft itself. Though **"Office Online"** no longer exists, you can still search the company's database of free clip-art and photographs. From any Office app (not just PowerPoint) go to the Insert menu and choose "Online Pictures" (as shown below):

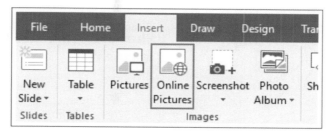

The search engine this button produces is powered by Bing, and it's more powerful than the original Office search engine. For the free stuff, choose "CC Only" (Creative Commons). Wider searches are available, but many of those results may be copyrighted for commercial (paid) use only. Until you get used to it, it's worth spending a little time to familiarize yourself with the various license categories. You still might have to look very hard to find just the right piece, but generally you can snag something that is both professional and appropriate to your needs (and affordable if not free).

It's important, however, to correct the misconception that *all* clip-art is bad and should never be used. Instead, it's more accurate to say that:

a. a lot of clip-art is cheesy and/or immature and/or poorly drawn

b. some clip-art is downright wonderful (see below)

c. if used, clip-art should fit audience, occasion, and mood

d. by definition, clip-art is a more **whimsical** choice than photographic images, so always weigh its appropriateness

Thankfully, a careful search of sites like Shutterstock suggests that the olden days of neon green money and sky-blue sweaters are numbered:

Shutterstock Image ID 83419651

Shutterstock Image ID 17636251

Shutterstock Image ID 91692797

Choosing between clip-art and photographs depends on your analysis of the audience, your presentational goals, and other factors. But one thing is certain: Because slides are a visual medium, **they abso-freakin-lutely require the presence of graphic elements** to even have a shot at communicating your message effectively.

Good clip-Art? Fine. Photographs? Great. Neither? **You're asking for trouble.**

Text simply must not be allowed to not dominate or overpower your slides. As pointed out repeatedly in the discussion of Rule 2, if you need to be text-intensive, use the printed page.

Speaking of photos and clip-art, what do all too many of the photographs used in slide presentations have in common with the piece of clip-art shown here?

Answer: They're **grainy** ⎯⎯⎯⎯⎯⎯⎯⟶

While I'm not proud of that pun, if it got your attention then it was still worthwhile. And I can live with that.

Grainy and otherwise distorted images are the bane of slidewatching audiences everywhere. Take this, um, *blurry* stapler for instance:

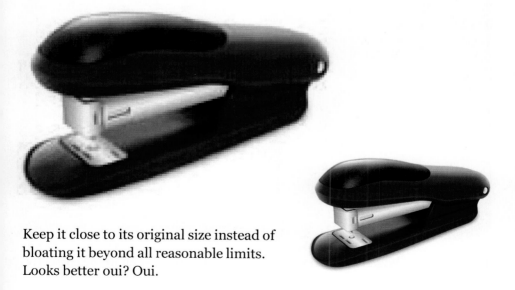

Keep it close to its original size instead of bloating it beyond all reasonable limits. Looks better oui? Oui.

If the original image is too small to work at larger sizes, don't push it. Just keep looking until you find one that will. Using quality images is Job One.

Speaking of too small, can you tell what's going on in the photo on the right? Perhaps, but try doing so:

- from 50 feet away
- in harsh lighting
- when it's only on screen for 3 seconds
- and this is *actual size*

Grainy is one thing, but it's no better than the alternative—an image that's too small for audience members to cognitively process. Next time you're sizing a photo for use in a presentation, just ask yourself: *What would Goldilocks do?* Presumably, she'd always pick the image that was "just right." Not too grainy. Not too small. Not on screen too briefly.

But making photos too big or too small instead of just right isn't the only pet peeve audiences have with slide images. For example, notice anything odd about this photo of a famous American landmark? Actually, there are two different problems—it is both stretched too far horizontally and compressed vertically.

Every straight-edged image has **eight** control points as seen in the correctly proportioned version of the photo shown at left on the next page:

However, to resize an image *and maintain its original proportionality, only the corner control points can be used* (see version at right). Dragging from any of the middle control points will produce an image that looks "squashed" or "stretched" or otherwise distorted.

Not all photographs give the appearance of having straight edges, however. Neither, for that matter, does most clip-art. The rules for dealing with such "edge-less" images will be discussed in a moment.

In the meantime, flip back and see if you notice anything about the straight-edged images that have appeared so far in this book. They've all had two distinct formatting techniques applied to them.

Can you figure out what they are?

To check your guesses, consider this photo that was imported (as is) from Shutterstock.

Like every other straight-edged image that gets put on a slide, this one needs just a couple of finishing touches:

- **1/4-point border**
- **Drop-shadow**

A one-quarter-point line is the smallest border available in slide programs, and it does the job without calling undue attention to itself. As for line color, go with black unless the image itself demands the use of a different color. Finally, be sure to crop the image if there are any gaps between the edges of the image and the border lines.

There are numerous variations on the basic idea of the shadow, but I almost always use the default lower-right drop shadow.

If we apply both of these simple techniques to our image of Mt. Fuji, we get first the left image (with border) and then the finished one on the right (with border and drop-shadow):

It is important to note, however, that not all images are meant to seem "framed" in this way. For example, look what happens when these three pieces are formatted with a border and shadow:

Such artificial borders serve no purpose (hence the exclamation marks). They just diminish the visual impact of the images they surround. With straight-edged photos like Mt. Fuji, a border "frames" the image and effectively gives it a formal, "finished" quality. Not so with open-ended images like our fire hydrant, bouquet, and kettle. Instead of framing and finishing, borders serve only to constrain them. If you have a slide with a white or very light background, leave "edge-less" images such as these unframed—they are most effective when allowed to naturally blend with the space around them.

That goes for a majority of traditional clip-art images as well (i.e., two-dimensional drawings). Don't run for a border. Just let them be:

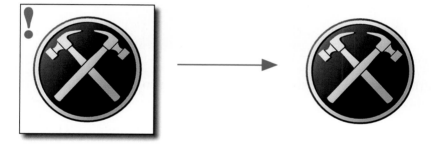

The ability to let such images blend in is a chief advantage of using templates with **white backgrounds** (as opposed to those with dark backgrounds). If this is not an option, however, the artificial fill color (white or otherwise) around the edges of many images can often be made to disappear using the "Set Transparent Color" option. (In Office for Windows, double click the graphic to call up the Picture Tools/Format ribbon. Look for "Recolor" at the far left, then drop down to find the option for setting transparent color.) The image can then blend into a slide of any background color.

Rule 5: **Color**

High Contrast

How many presentations have you sat through where it was ALMOST IMPOSSIBLE TO SEE the text. Even with the lights off? From the front row? Like this sample slide, for example:

The fifth Rule of Design exists because the answer to this question is inevitably "too many."

Surely most speakers don't intentionally torment their audiences by using weak color combinations. It happens so frequently that there has to be some other explanation.

Here's what's going on. When making slides, presenters are almost always looking at a **small screen**, be it a laptop display, a tablet, or a desktop monitor. But these devices all have **high-resolution**. As a result, even the poorest color combinations appear readable.

So as presenters create slides, it naturally doesn't occur to them that some color choices **might not translate well to big screen projection systems**.

The typical projection screen has a much lower resolution than a small monitor. Brightness is greatly diminished, as are the depth, richness, and number of colors. Thus slides often appear "washed out" on screen when compared to the vibrant colors that our small monitors produce.

Mercifully, the solution to this problem is simple. When making slides, presenters should compare the color of the **text** to the color of the **background** it's on. Check to ensure that one of two conditions is always true:

Dark text is against a light background

and/or:

Light text is against a dark background

As long as one of these conditions is true for every item of text on your slides, then by definition you're using a **high-contrast** color combination. As a result, no matter what the physical condition of the venue you're presenting in—overhead lighting, projector quality, etc.—more likely than not, the audience will be able to read the text on your slides unless it's in something like 12-point Times New Roman. And in that case, you're already your own worst enemy.

Just think of it. No more vain attempts to decipher:

yellow text on a white background

gray text on a black background

white text on a cyan background

red text on a brown(ish) background

Text colors and background colors should be VERY whatever they are—
namely **very** dark or **very** light, and each the opposite of the other (one
dark, the other light).

But beware the temptation to classify BRIGHT colors as LIGHT ones.
Visually, they're different parameters—one has to do with hue, the other
with saturation. **Do not put bright colors on top of each other.**

Keep **bright text** colors and **bright background** colors AWAY from each
other. Combining them produces a bizarre visual phenomenon known as:

Simultaneous contrast

And in case you were wondering, it "works" the other way too:

Simultaneous contrast

Don't merely glance. **Stare** at both of these boxes for a while.

The reason the text in these swatches appears to be "buzzing" is this—our brains don't know whether the red or the blue belongs in the foreground. As a result, we're assigning **both** colors to the foreground *at the same time.* By the way, it's bad enough here in a staring contest with a printed page, but try these combinations for real the next time you're making slides (or on your computer right now if you're so inclined). The effects are much more pronounced on actual screens. One thing's for sure: It would certainly make a memorable attention getter for your next presentation. Just not in the way you were hoping.

Before we get to the last two Rules of Design, let's recap:

1. **Templates and Themes:** Choose wisely

2. **Text:** Reining in Wordiness

3. **Fonts:** Use Sans Serif Typefaces

4. **Images:** Keep It Classy

5. **Color:** High Contrast

Now, take your newfound knowledge of this rule and the previous four and use it to critique the slide in the exercise that follows.

Brace yourself. It's a doozy.

Putting It All Together

Consider this slide, the cringe-inducing design of which is, unfortunately, all-too-familiar:

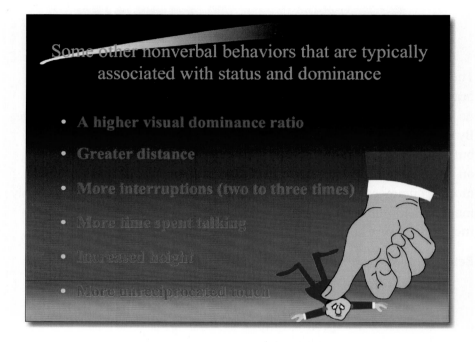

Scary, ain't it? Well its atrocious stylings are the pride and joy of my good friend and graduate school mentor, who deliberately breaks all of the Rules of Design just to irritate me. To make up for that, it was his idea to base this exercise on one of his slides.

Study this slide in light of the first five Rules of Design presented in this book, then on the following page list all of the things that are wrong with it (in any order). Note that there probably aren't 15 separate things wrong with this slide, but you never know. Besides, we had the room to put 15 lines on the next page, so we did.

Happy hunting.

1. _____

2. _____

3. _____

4. _____

5. _____

6. _____

7. _____

8. _____

9. _____

10. _____

11. _____

12. _____

13. _____

14. _____

15. _____

Rule 6: **Animation**

Easy Does It

When we were growing up and our moms encouraged us to be creative, going bonkers with the endless animation possibilities inherent in electronic slides was not what they had in mind. And while I've never actually met your Mom, trust me when I say that she agrees with everything I'm about to say.

Consider the following philosophical questions. Had he thought of it first, I'm sure Plato would have christened this the "Art thou really, truly certain of that?" method:

- Do we really need to see what a line of text looks like

  ... ***backwards***
  ... while ***spinning***?

REALLY?

Do we really need to see text come ***bouncing*** in one word (or, Heaven help us, one letter) at a time, like Jack Russell puppies hopped up on catnip?

REALLY?

- Do we really need to ... Oh my gosh! That text is ... is ***zooming***. *It's coming right for us!*

REALLY?

- Do we really need to see things ***fly in*** from here, there, and everywhere, for the umpteenth time?

REALLY?

Mayday!

Speaking of Plato, he is believed by some people to be the source of the following gem of slide design wisdom. If so, he was way ahead of his time:

Animation effects
should REVEAL things
not REVEL in them.

Good design only REVEALS content; it never REVELS in it. Reveling is for life, for love, for parties, and for puppies. Not for bullets on a presentation screen. Recall the principle of transparency, meaning that good design does not draw undue attention to itself. That means no flying, crazy zooming, bouncing, fencing, or basket weaving.

In fact, for the record, audiences the world over would like to **prohibit** bullets, text boxes, and most other slide-based objects from engaging in **any** of the following activities. To do so should be considered a perversion of the electronic order:

As the preceding list suggests, the general rule for evaluating animation effects is this:

If it moves, SHOOT it.

Unless you **need** to move an object, choose animation effects that don't require your content to change ZIP codes in order to get where it's going. A little animation is one thing, but MOVEMENT is something else entirely. Animation effects that feature a significant amount of screen movement are **distracting**.

Recently the FBI may (or may not) have published their "**10 Most Unwanted**" list for animation effects. Not surprisingly, "Fly In" was Public Animation Enemy Number 1. And it's in good company. Here's the complete list:

1. **Fly In**
2. Crawl In
3. Swivel
4. Bounce
5. Spiral In
6. Center Revolve
7. Rise Up
8. Boomerang

9. Magnify
10. Fold
11. Float
12. Light Speed
13. Credits
14. Flip
15. Swish
16. Pinwheel

Sixteen items on a Top 10 list? Apparently, the FBI needs more accountants. By the way, even though **Fly In** is the worst offender on the list by virtue of its being abused far more than any other, make no mistake: Using any of these motion-based effects to animate text is a bad idea.

Why specifically? They violate the prime directive of good design mentioned previously—transparency—by calling the audience's attention to the effect rather than the content. **Good design never competes with its own content for the audience's attention.** In addition, there are three more good reasons not to use these kinds of effects for handling text:

1. **AMATEURISH:** Such choices suggest that the speaker isn't terribly experienced—an attribution that no presenter can afford. It's an instant credibility-shrinker for the speaker, and, for the audience, an instant enthusiasm-shrinker.

2. **UNPROFESSIONAL:** Even worse than looking like an amateur, seeming unprofessional communicates something else to the audience—something quite unintended but also quite damaging: **disrespect**. No presenter can afford that.

3. **TIME CONSUMING:** Audiences don't want (or deserve) to wait while our bullets c-r-a-w-l across the screen. Also, as speakers, what are we supposed to do during this time "in transit"—tell jokes? (Did you hear the one about the two text boxes who walked into a bar chart?)

At this point, of course, we're ready to ask the obvious question—what are the characteristics of GOOD animation effects? There are three things to look for:

1. **LOW-KEY:** The effect does not call attention to itself

2. **STATIONARY:** Minimal left/right or up/down movement

3. **QUICK:** Wastes no time—the audience's or yours

Unless you have a good reason not to, use the "**Fade**" effect set at "**Very fast**" speed. That said, if I'm feeling the love and/or have had too much cough syrup, I will occasionally allow myself to use the following:

- Expand
- Compress
- Ascend
- Descend
- Wipe

> ## ACHTUNG, BABY!
> **All guidelines mentioned in this chapter apply equally to entrance and <u>exit</u> effects alike**

- Strips
- Split

There are other acceptable choices that still manage to meet the three criteria above, but it's hard to go wrong with any of these listed. And as the box above suggests, IF you need to use **exit** effects (I'm not saying that you do), these devices still represent your best stable of choices.

Having come so far, however, there is still **one final warning** to heed lest all your hard work and excellent choices amount to naught:

Sound effects (not actual audio but the built-in bells, horns, etc.)

They're not helpful

They're annoying

Do not use them

No explosions

No drum rolls

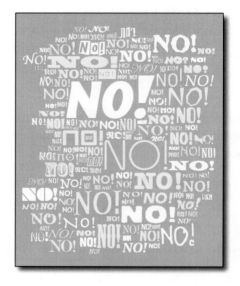

No cha-chings

No gunshots

No tires peeling

No camera clicks

No chimes

No clapping

No breaking glass

No applause (other than what you earn from the audience).

ANIMATION

- ## Do I need to use animation effects at all?

  Definitely. Using entrance effects puts you in control of the narrative, and, as speaker, that's your job. Don't let the audience pick and choose where to direct their attention. This isn't Craigslist or window shopping. It's a live guided tour and you're the tour guide. By not using entrance effects to introduce talking points, you risk having the audience read ahead and get distracted by something you haven't even had the chance to put into context yet.

- ## So I should use entrance effects. What about exit effects?

  Exit effects aren't generally necessary. Once you've introduced your talking points, leaving them in place is useful because it helps audiences remember the overall narrative and how its various parts fit together. However, this notion only applies to text. If you have a lot of IMAGES to cycle through on a given slide, then using exit effects to avoid clutter is a necessity.

- ## What about dimming bullets as you move down a list?

  Better than exiting them off-screen altogether, but still not recommended. Audiences are pretty darn good at keeping up with you. And even though it seems counterintuitive, there's something about dimming bullets that makes some audience members want to "go back" and see what they missed—almost as if you're daring them to do so. If that happens then you're well on your way to losing control of the presentation.

ANIMATION

- ## Is using a variety of animation effects in a presentation okay?

  You can, if you wish, use different effects for different categories of objects—for example: Fade for text bullets, Descend for standalone text boxes, and Faded Zoom for images. But within a category, strive for consistency. A consistent visual style can't be overrated as it's an attribute that speaks directly to your professionalism, and hence your credibility as a presenter.

- ## Are the animation rules different for images?

  A little bit. First, it's worth noting that Fade and the other recommended effects work just as well for images as they do for bullets and text boxes, so don't stray from them unless you just can't help it. And if you just can't help it, don't venture much beyond Zoom, Faded Zoom, or Grow and Turn. As mentioned above, it's often a good idea to use exit effects when working with multiple images on a slide in order to prevent clutter, and to manage the narrative more efficiently. However, having said all that, one prohibition remains inviolate: No Fly In or Fly Out effect.

- ## What about using random effects?

  Sure. As long as you're into playing Russian Roulette with your audience's nerves.

- ## Why would Microsoft put most of the offending effects under a category called "Exciting"?

  It's either the height of irony or a typo. Here's my theory: One day at Microsoft, a programmer became distracted by a text message or a low-flying plane, glanced away from the computer, and inadvertently omitted four letters while trying to type the word "Excruciating."

Rule 7: cApiTaLIzaTiOn

Dial It Back

Shakespeare has had many famous phrases attributed to him. One saying that has not been attributed to him (yet) is the following:

To capitalize or not to capitalize.

That is the question.

In fact, it's the question we face every time we type a title, a bullet of text, or a single word in a box. The answer, which may come as a surprise to many, is **NO** most of the time.

Just as in other media—writing, for instance—capital letters are a special case (pardon the pun) that are only used to confer status on a few words in a given passage. Consider this excerpt from Lewis Carroll's timeless classic, rendered the way we normally would in English, using what's called "Sentence" case capitalization:

> "In THAT direction," the Cat said, waving its right paw round, "lives a Hatter: and in THAT direction," waving the other paw, "lives a March Hare. Visit either you like: they're both mad."

There are 33 words in this passage. Of these, exactly eight are capitalized, including two made entirely of capitals. This means that only about 25% of the words have special status, conferred on the basis of position (first word), need for emphasis, or rank (proper nouns). Without such built-in differentiation, **meaning would be obscured**, and readers would have to **work harder** to interpret the author's original intent. For example:

"in that direction," the cat said, waving its right paw round, "lives a hatter: and in that direction," waving the other paw, "lives a march hare. visit either you like: they're both mad."

Just doesn't have the same punch, does it? Not a problem if you're texting someone, but definitely less than desirable in more formal settings. But just as there's more than one way to skin a Cheshire Cat, there's more than one way to misuse capitalization in ways that obscure meaning. Have another look. This is called "Start" case, but if you're using it, please "Stop"—

"In THAT Direction," The Cat Said, Waving Its Right Paw Round, "Lives A Hatter: And In THAT Direction," Waving The Other Paw, "Lives A March Hare. Visit Either You Like: They're Both Mad."

In Start case, every word is capitalized (shudder). As a result, the entire thing looks like one big title, not a paragraph of prose. None of us would ever write a paragraph this way—and yet **people do it all the time on slides**. Not only is Start case actually harder to read than all lowercase, it also renders the very idea of capitals meaningless. This observation is important enough to merit its own colored box:

If Everything Is Capitalized, Capital Letters Mean Nothing

If this is our approach to capitalization, there's no point bothering with it at all. The idea of special status goes out the window. We need some words to be more important than others, at least visually, in order to communicate more effectively.

And don't confuse Start case with "Title" case. We love Title case, which caps the first word and everything else EXCEPT prepositions, conjunctions, and articles. For example, in 1984 Douglas Adams published the fourth book in his *Hitchhiker* series, and because he used Title case it looks correct to our eye:

Save Our Slides

So Long, and Thanks for All the Fish

Not capitalized: prepositions, conjunctions, and articles

But there is still one more possible iteration of capitalization we need to explore, namely the practice of ALL-CAPPING:

"IN THAT DIRECTION," THE CAT SAID, WAVING ITS RIGHT PAW ROUND, "LIVES A HATTER: AND IN THAT DIRECTION," WAVING THE OTHER PAW, "LIVES A MARCH HARE. VISIT EITHER YOU LIKE: THEY'RE BOTH MAD."

Once again, the value of capitalization as a communication strategy is negated. All-capping is also extremely hard on the eyes—and the brain. That's because we read English words largely on the basis of appearance— the distinctive shapes produced when lowercase letters combine with the occasional uppercase. Lowercase letters are easier to distinguish from one another than uppercase letters are from other uppercase letters, as can be seen easily enough in this comparison:

a b c d e f g h i j k l m n o p q r s t u v w x y z

A B C D E F G H I J K L M N O P Q R S T U V W X Y Z

Some uppercase letters share similar shapes, making them harder to differentiate as individual characters (like K and X, for example), and hence harder to read. For instance, consider the following list of three goals that many troubled organizations might aspire to, and hence use as a slide at a meeting. Here it is in Arial typeface. Decide for yourself which approach looks better:

- Recoup core crop
- Regroup web code
- Regrow proud force

- RECOUP CORE CROP
- REGROUP WEB CODE
- REGROW PROUD FORCE

Save Our Slides

If you're at a computer, try the same experiment. You'll find the difference even more noticeable. Using all-caps occasionally for EMPHASIS is fine ("Regrow PROUD force"), but as with all forms of emphasis (underlining, bolding, etc.) one should use all-caps SPARINGLY.

So what's a slidemaker to do? Now that you know some of the lingo and the theory behind it, applying the following rules is a straightforward proposition:

1. **For Slide Titles Use Title Case**

2. **For main bullets use Sentence case**

3. **In sub-bullets capitalize proper nouns only**

4. **For SPECIAL emphasis only, use all-caps as needed**

To illustrate these rules, consider the two slides below. Which one is correct? And which one looks better? (Trick question: the correct slide should also look better).

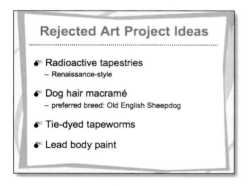

Here they are again, larger this time and with commentary to point out the differences:

☑ Correct

Rejected Art Project Ideas

- Radioactive tapestries
  - Renaissance-style
- Dog hair macramé
  - preferred breed: Old English Sheepdog
- Tie-dyed tapeworms
- Lead body paint

Title Case:
Every word capitalized <u>except</u> for prepositions, conjunctions, articles, and small land animals.

Sentence Case:
Capitalize <u>only</u> first word and <u>proper</u> nouns. Use ALL-CAPS for special emphasis only.

Sub-bullets:
ONLY proper nouns are capitalized. This rule also applies to the first word of the line. ALL-CAPS okay for special emphasis only.

⃠ Incorrect

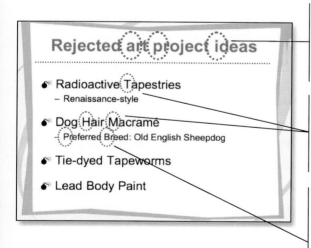

Rejected art project ideas

- Radioactive Tapestries
  - Renaissance-style
- Dog Hair Macramé
  - Preferred Breed: Old English Sheepdog
- Tie-dyed Tapeworms
- Lead Body Paint

Mistake:
Using Sentence case in the title is too informal. Titles should look like titles not sentences.

Boo-boo:
As the keyworded remnants of full sentences, only first word and proper nouns should be capitalized.

Ouchie:
At sub-bullet level, ONLY proper nouns are capitalized. By definition sub-bullets are <u>less</u> important than main bullets and this should be reflected visually.

CAPITALIZATION, etc.

- **What about punctuation on slides?**

  Take another look at the previous slides and note one more correct design attribute they both share in common—a decided lack of punctuation. **Bullets and sub-bullets are keywords—not actual sentences. As a result, we don't owe them any punctuation.** Visually, adding periods to bullets and sub-bullets simply increases a slide's clutter—something we're trying to produce less of not more.

  Note well that ending periods are OUT. Keywords eliminate the need for them.

  The occasional question mark is okay if in fact you're asking a question. Question marks are best used, however, if the main bullets (or the sub-bullets) on a given slide are **all** phrased as questions.

  The occasional internal comma is fine if you're listing things, but avoid having terminal commas hanging at the end of lines.

  Also, exclamation marks are a bad idea! Really! Avoid them! They make you look desperate! Amateurish! Unprofessional! And jittery!

- **Is it okay to combine all-caps and bolding to give extra special emphasis to a particular word?**

  Sure, but don't get carried away. As special words go, anything you double-up on like that better be pretty spectacularly important.

CAPITALIZATION, etc.

- ## Is it strictly necessary to capitalize the first word of main bullets?

  Not strictly, no, because main bullets are not actual sentences, only the keyworded vestiges of them. If your own personal style demands it, feel free to leave those first words lowercase— unless, of course, they're proper nouns. Three caveats, however:

  One, realize that the vast majority of presenters do it the way I described in this chapter, so doing otherwise may look a little odd to your audience, and that means you're taking the risk of distracting them.

  Two, whatever visual style you adopt when it comes to capitalization, be consistent from slide to slide to slide.

  Three, not capitalizing the first word of a bullet conveys a more informal sense than using traditional Sentence case does. Hence, if formality is inherent in the context of your presentation, then you're better off sticking with the approach described in this chapter.

Stand and Deliver

- Position yourself as shown below
- Talk to the audience, not to the screen
- Use the screen as you would a notecard—for reference only

Face the audience, at a slight angle

Turn your head, not your body, to glance at the screen. Facing the audience will force you to turn your head back to face them frequently.

Your shoulders form a straight line to the center of the screen

Body Talk

- Default hand position:
  - **Up, together, in front of your chest**
  - **Place one thumb in the opposite palm**
- From there, it's easy to **gesture**, **gesture**, **gesture**
- Always come back to this default position between gestures

Do NOT put your hands:

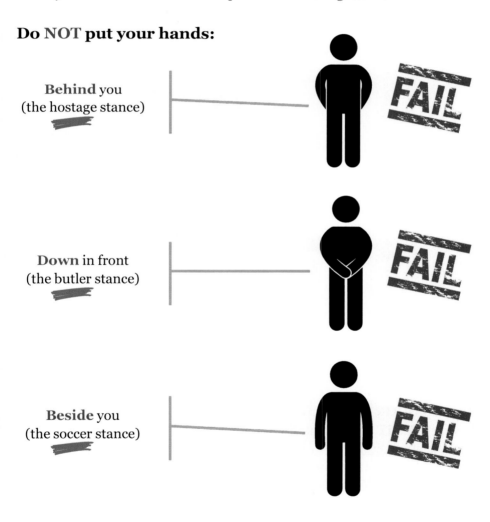

Behind you
(the hostage stance)

Down in front
(the butler stance)

Beside you
(the soccer stance)

Hide and Seek

If you need to **blank** the screen in order to better manage a conversation with the audience, there are two easy options, the B key or the W key.

The B key blacks out the screen.

The W key whites it out.

Click any key or press the mouse button and the blank screen disappears.

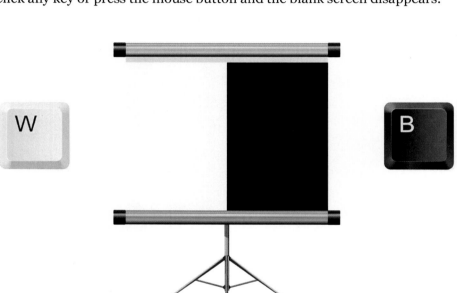

To jump **DIRECTLY** to any slide **WITHOUT** having to **EXIT** the presentation, simply type the <u>page number of that slide</u> + the Enter key. Just make sure you have a printed index listing the numbers and titles of every slide (unless you happen to have that memorized). Doing so takes the guesswork out of this direct navigation technique.

Video Victory

Audiences are quite accepting of grainy, poor-quality video (thank you, World Wide Web). This paradox is great news for presenters because it means that, as long as the subject and content of the video is fitting, almost any clip can enhance the impact of a presentation.

There is only one caveat here: **It has to actually work**. If the video doesn't play, loses audio, hangs up, etc., then you risk looking unprepared, unprofessional, or even incompetent. The best way to avoid such snafus is to use a **physical video file** rather than trying to link to or embed code from a video that resides online somewhere.

Assuming you aren't in violation of copyright and/or fair use laws, your chosen clip is best in one of the following slide-friendly video formats:

- **avi** (Windows Video File)
- **wmv** (Windows Media Video)
- **mov** (Quicktime—Mac users only)

ONE MORE THING: **Any video clip "inserted" on a slide must be present as a separate file alongside your presentation.** Despite appearances, the videos <u>aren't actually contained</u> IN your slides. What looks like a video on a slide is just a placeholder that points to where the file of the actual video resides.

There are other potentially compatible file types, but choosing them means potentially playing with fire. If you need to convert an existing video into .avi or .wmv format, consider using a program like **Microsoft Expression Encoder**. Mac users, to create .wmv files you need to install the **Flip4Mac** QuickTime video codecs. Installing the codecs for *viewing* .wmv files is free, but to *convert* such files into .mov format (or vice versa) may require a software purchase. But beware: If you download one of those "free" converters, watch out for the toolbars, applets, and adware that they sometimes try to surreptitiously install on your computer.

Auto In-correct

By default, PowerPoint tries to be helpful in a variety of ways by guessing what it's just *sure* you were going to do anyway and then pre-emptively doing it for you. As my friend Mo would ask sardonically at this point:

"What could possibly go wrong?"

Oooooh, a couple of things, as it turns out. Namely, automatically resizing text and titles in order to "make room" for new content you're trying to add to an existing slide. Here's how to tell PowerPoint to stop deciding such things for you.

1. Find the program's "**Options**" function (under "File" in Windows)

2. Then choose "**Proofing**" and click "**AutoCorrect Options** ..."

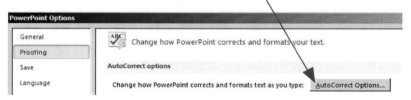

3. Almost there! Click the tab "**AutoFormat As You Type**"—

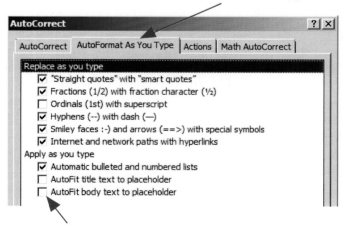

4. It's only the **last two items** on this list that we're concerned about

5. **Uncheck them!**

6. They're checked by default, so unless someone else uses your computer, it's unlikely you'll find them turned off. If they *are* already off when you get there, it might be time to find out who else has been touching your stuff.

While you're at it, click the "AutoCorrect" tab

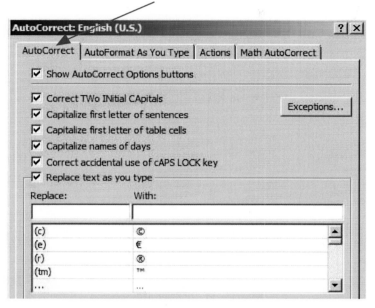

This will assure that there isn't some other thing that PowerPoint is doing for you that you'd rather do yourself.

And don't worry. This type of thing can't be counted against you when people try to bring up your control issues. Usually.

Beautiful Bookends

Every slideshow needs nice front and back covers, or what I call "bookend" slides.

If nothing else, you can use the traditional title slide layout that comes with your template to type a title and subtitle.

Click to add title

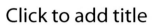
Click to add subtitle

Meh. Color me and Boss Hogg the Dogg relatively unimpressed.

While technically better than nothing, this approach is so commonplace and pedestrian it truly could bore a dog. And if a dog can be bored by it, imagine how your audience is likely to feel.

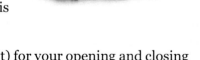

Instead, let go of the template (just ignore it) for your opening and closing cover slides and use **stunning full-screen images** instead.

Think of them as the **glossy front and back covers** of a brochure or a beautiful set of bookends bracketing items on a shelf (sorry about all of the Bs in this sentence). When done well, they give presentations a "finished" look, subtly conveying to your audience that you put some real effort into this presentation. The attitudinal differences in the way your audience perceives you and your message are probably impossible to measure, but they're there and they're real.

So, how about some better approaches? Let's assume you're part of a company or organization named "LOREM," and this spiffy blue-green thing is your logo or symbol.

Whether the background is light or dark doesn't matter in this context. In fact, a black or dark bookend can be striking and memorable. Remember, this is a cover slide, not a template, so using a dark background color is just fine.

At the end of the presentation, just use the same cover slide again (hence the term "bookends"). Bring up the closing bookend slide when you say your goodbyes and thank-yous or move into a question-and-answer session. **Never just END a presentation on your last content slide.**

Of course, you could get a little more creative if the occasion merits. Should the subject of your presentation have something to do with transportation, for example, consider using a pair of complementary bookends that visually imply coming and going:

Infusing your bookends with this kind of visual logic is an opportunity to creatively grab and hold an audience's attention. That said, such an approach is inherently more whimsical than simply showing the logo at the beginning and end. So, make sure that whatever you do fits the occasion. Here's hoping you'll have an opportunity to use a visual pairing like this sometime:

It's Transition Time

There are actually two kinds of transitions that presenters often overlook. One type is **visual** and super easy to do. The other kind is **verbal** and unique to the content of a given presentation. Super important, but not particularly easy.

By "visual transitions" what I officially mean is **visual transitions between slides**. And in PowerPoint specifically there's only one as far as I'm concerned. Under "**Transitions**" choose "**Fade**" then go to "**Effect Options ▼**," and select "**Through Black**" as (sort of) shown here:

And, yes, there are other transition effects, but they tend to draw too much attention to themselves.

But there is one last thing. BEFORE selecting this effect, **highlight all of your slides**. This step is illustrated on the next page using a sample presentation about ancient buildings. And while you're at it, be sure to check out those awesome, avant-garde bookend slides.

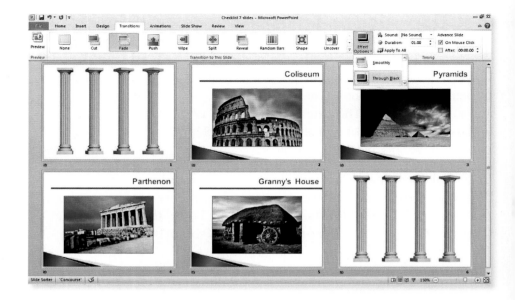

Visual transitions impart a sense of connectedness to the slides in a presentation, allowing each one to flow smoothly into the next. As it turns out, **verbal transitions** do the same thing for the **ideas** contained in those slides. Only they're a lot harder to implement.

First, understand that words and phrases like **next, moving on, in addition, now then,** and **also** do <u>not</u> constitute meaningful verbal transitions.

The **main ideas in your body** need to be connected by **meaningful** verbal transitions—logical bridges that explain how we got from the previous slide to the current slide. I'm NOT talking about getting from your introduction to your first main idea or from your last main idea to the closing. Those are technical verbal transitions that tend to take care of themselves (e.g., "to begin" and "in closing").

Rather, how does Main Idea 1 **connect logically** to Main Idea 2 and how does Main Idea 2 **connect logically** to Main Idea 3? And so on. Unfortunately, you'd be surprised at how often these important elements are simply omitted.

Save Our Slides

But it's a big challenge for presenters. After all, if speakers can't clearly articulate the connection between main ideas/slides, why should they expect it to be obvious to their audience?

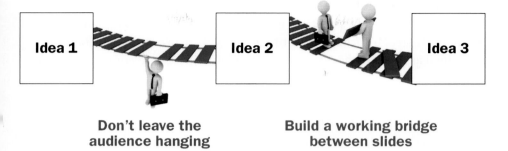

Don't leave the audience hanging

Build a working bridge between slides

It's practically a given that there exists some kind of meaningful relationship between any two ideas in the same speech. And that's the key. Find the relationship and use it as the basis for the verbal transition. Relationships are many and varied. Don't limit yourself to **cause-and-effect** (unless of course it's the right answer). Consider these other formal relationships as well:

- **Time** (including before/after)
- **Antithesis** (opposition, including compare/contrast)
- **General-to-specific** (or vice versa)
- **Problem-solution**
- **Increasing superiority** (or vice versa)
- **Spatial** (including geography)

Suppose you're talking about a company with three seemingly unrelated divisions: office supplies, sporting goods, and organic foods. Depending on the specific details of the scenario, you could, for example, contrast the performance of the office supplies division with the sporting goods division, or you could arrange all three in order from poorest performance to the best performance. If a relationship doesn't present itself eventually, then try rearranging the order of the slides/ideas. In the end, you don't have to link all of your main ideas directly to each other, you simply have to find the bridge that gets you from one slide to the next in a logical and meaningful way.

About the Author

Dr. William "Billy" Earnest is an Assistant Professor of Communication at St. Edward's University in Austin, Texas. He has Ph.D. and Master's degrees from The University of Texas at Austin, where he taught as an Assistant Instructor from 1997 until 2001. Not surprisingly, his doctoral work focused on the effectiveness of electronic slides as a communication medium.

From 2002 to 2005 he was on the faculty of UT's prestigious McCombs School of Business, where he lectured in Business Communication. While there, he was nominated for a Texas Exes Outstanding Teaching Award.

Courses he has taught regularly include:

- Media and Professional Presentations
- Business Communication
- Persuasion
- Presentational Speaking
- Intercultural Communication
- Lying and Deception in Human Interaction

Billy hails from Wichita Falls, Texas, home of his Alma Mater, Midwestern State University. From 1990 to 1995, he was an Atlanta-based systems analyst, technical writer, and corporate trainer for Electronic Data Systems.

He and his 95-lb. ball of furry joy, Dylan D. Dawg, are proud to live in South Austin. In 2015, he and Dylan made their first meme, shown here.